CONTENDING
for the
FAITH

David R. Barnhart

Other books by David R. Barnhart:
The Church's Desperate Need for Revival
Israel Land of Promise and Prophecy

A study guide, featuring 12 sessions, has been prepared for use with *Contending for the Faith*. It is especially appropriate for adult Sunday school classes and Bible-study groups.

Also available: **The Vine and Branches,** a newsletter, edited by David R. Barnhart, offering timely articles relating to current events in the church. Write for a free copy.

Abiding Word Ministries
4300 Nicols Road
Eagan, Minnesota 55122

CONTENDING
for the
FAITH

David R. Barnhart

Abiding Word Publications
Eagan, Minnesota

DEDICATION

To my grandchildren and their grandchildren,
my personal reasons —
"to earnestly contend for the faith
which was once delivered unto the saints."

ACKNOWLEDGEMENTS

I am grateful to Anna Marie Gardner for her invaluable assistance in editing this book; to Pastor William Tweeddale for writing the foreword and giving me so much encouragement throughout this project; and to my wife Mary, whose support and counsel made this book possible. My special thanks to my daughter-in-law, Sylvia Eggers Barnhart, for her sketch of Archangel Michael's conquest of Satan that appears on the front cover. Lastly, my thanks to the hymn-writers of the past whose music still inspires the church to contend for the faith with joy and gladness.

Contents

Foreword   by William F. Tweeddale viii

Chapter 1   Contending for the Faith
     — the Challenge 1

Chapter 2   Contending for the Faith
     — our Duty 9

Chapter 3   Contending for the Faith
     — of our Fathers 19

Chapter 4   Contending for the Faith
     — not Denominational Distinctives 31

Chapter 5   Contending for the Faith
     — and the Word of God 43

Chapter 6   Contending for the Faith
     — Watchful for Subtle Deceptions 59

Chapter 7   Contending for the Faith
     — and Biblical Morality 75

Chapter 8   Contending for the Faith
     — Against the One-World Religion 105

Chapter 9   Contending for the Faith
     — Against the One-World Government 133

Chapter 10   Contending for the Faith
     — Against the Feminist Onslaught 149

Chapter 11   Contending for the Faith
     — Pathways to Victory 169

Chapter 12   Contending for the Faith
     — Encouragement for Battle-Weary Christians 193

Foreword

David R. Barnhart makes us aware that we are not alone in the struggle for truth. Many of us have lived through the trauma of seeing the ancient boundaries moved. We remember the security and gentleness of a society that assumed Christianity was the model for our nation. We watched the bastion of truth fall to the onslaught of humanism. America's motto, "In God We Trust," no longer holds sway as people gravitate instead to man as the "master of his fate, the captain of his soul." Once on this slippery slope, there was no stopping society's descent into paganism. Values have shifted to the point where we now protect the egg of a vulture and condone the killing of infants in the haven of their mothers' wombs. The pagan tyranny, once feared by Americans, is now happily embraced as we "worship and serve the creature more than the Creator ..." Romans 1:25).

Just when we thought all was lost, that the church had not only fallen asleep but also shriveled up into a lifeless force, God raised up another voice to call us back — back to the God-fearing ways of Scripture. David Barnhart stands shoulder to shoulder with a small army of men and women who are saying "no" to religion which has sold out to the sensual passions of mankind, sold out to the feminists who would take the liberty of changing the very Word of God to suit their agenda.

Today's religion has moved so far from honoring the Bible that it is nearly impossible to find an affirmation of biblical inerrancy in any statement of faith of a major denominational seminary. Young people are being trained for the ministry in our churches without ever knowing that the claims of the Bible have never been seriously challenged in academic debate, but simply cast aside because the Scriptures stood in the way of the liberals' hedonistic agenda.

This book should be read wherever there is a truly inquiring mind. It should be read by young people who are looking forward to a life of Christian service; it should be read by parents who want a defense against the senseless slaughter of their children by people who sneer at the word "chastity." This book should be read by men who stand behind the pulpits of our land wondering why their voices are not heard.

This is a clarion call for action — action that will follow the Word of God wherever it may lead us. David Barnhart has learned well the meaning of Martin Luther's battle cry, "sola Scriptura" (the Scriptures alone). Luther's stand for truth, which brought him close to the jaws of death but never close to surrender, has given courage to all who enter the arena to *contend for the faith*. Therefore, it is only fitting that a Lutheran should take up the baton and continue the race.

William F. Tweeddale
Grace Brethren Church
Melbourne, Florida

If I profess with the loudest voice and clearest exposition every point of the truth of God except precisely that little point which the world and the devil are at the moment attacking, I am not confessing Christ, however boldly I may be professing Christ. When the battle rages, there the loyalty of the soldier is proved and to be steady on all the battle front besides, is mere flight and disgrace if he flinches at that point.

Martin Luther

Chapter 1

Contending for the Faith — the Challenge

Preach the Word; be instant in season, out of season; reprove, rebuke, exhort with all longsuffering and doctrine. For the time will come when they will not endure sound doctrine; but after their own lusts shall they heap to themselves teachers, having itching ears; and they shall turn away their ears from the truth, and shall be turned unto fables (2 Timothy 4:2-4).

A fierce battle for the soul of the church is raging. Basic Christian beliefs are under attack. Congregations of every size, locality and denominational persuasion are targets of this assault. Many have fallen. The enemy has seized most mainline seminaries; he has even captured whole denominations. Observant church people express amazement at the extent of Satan's territorial conquests, recognizing that the battle for the church has intensified significantly in recent years.

Satan grows desperate to gain allies and conquer more strongholds as the Lord's return draws nearer. Fifty years ago, only a few pastors and congregations had gone over to the enemy. Today they are legion. It is increasingly difficult to find pastors in mainline churches who believe the Bible is truly God's Word. Compromising clergy bear a great responsibility for the impoverished spiritual condition of both the modern church and society. One day they will be required to answer for their reckless leadership over the flocks they were instructed to "guard."

THE ATTACK AGAINST THE WORD OF GOD

The description of the Bible as inspired, infallible and inerrant, once acknowledged as an unalterable article of faith, has been stricken from denominational and congregational constitutions by subterfuge and

1

deceit. Naive church members who thought their constitutions had been changed to accommodate a merger have discovered that church leaders foisted a revised version of Christianity upon them.

Scholars of historical criticism have mutilated the Bible and destroyed the faith of countless young people in church colleges, universities and seminaries. It is doubtful that you could find more than a handful of teachers in mainline church colleges or seminaries (the Southern Baptist Convention and the Lutheran Church-Missouri Synod being the exceptions) who believe in the inerrancy of Scripture, though this was a foundational doctrine of Protestantism through the middle of the present century. Liberal theologians have pooled their unbelieving ignorance to rewrite the Scriptures in conformity with their perverted, twisted theologies. Numerous church bodies have rejected the Bible as the final authority for all issues of faith and life. Denominational leaders and church conventions now demand the last word regarding theology and morality.

THE ATTACK AGAINST BIBLICAL MORALITY

Lines of decency are being erased. There is an unmistakable correlation between the nation's moral slide and the church's doctrinal slide. Today both church and society face an unprecedented moral crisis. Abortion, juvenile delinquency, drug addiction, alcoholism, crime, pornography and sexual permissiveness bear witness to the church's failure to impact the nation with God's law and gospel. Moreover, society's perverse values are increasingly tolerated and promoted within the churches. Some evils have gained acceptance, not in spite of the church, but because of the church.

Church doors have opened wide to receive homosexuals, bisexuals, transvestites and transsexuals, sin and all, in the name of inclusiveness. These inclusive churches make no attempt to call persons who engage in sexual perversions to repentance and faith in Christ. Instead, homosexuals are invited to teach Sunday school, lead youth programs, write educational materials and kneel before church altars to solemnize their "marriages." Ordained homosexuals and their supporters are welcomed into the pulpits of American churches where they preach their sin-sick gospel of tolerance for every perverted lifestyle.

The divorce rate among mainline clergy is at an all-time high. Some

2

pastors have affairs, divorce their wives, remarry, and never miss a Sunday in their pulpits. It is not unusual to hear of pastors or denominational leaders being charged with moral misconduct of the most depraved nature, even in Bible-believing churches.

Bible-denying denominations mimic society by embracing worldly values. Within weeks of some social upheaval or a newly discovered oppressed minority, mainline denominations rush to draft statements in order to make the church body appear relevant in a changing society. Their church conventions often resemble Sodom and Gomorrah with homosexuals promoting their causes and distributing literature. In one mainline denomination, condoms were distributed to delegates at a synod convention to promote "safe sex." Liberal church conventions regularly adopt positions that violate biblical teachings. They have enacted statements and policies on nearly every social issue imaginable, except for the most important one of all — reaching the lost with the gospel of Jesus Christ. Few worry over that, however, since doctrines of universalism and cooperation with non-Christian religions have all but rendered the Great Commission of Christ null and void in their churches.

THE ATTACK AGAINST TRUTH

Mainline denominations, with few exceptions, have watered down or abandoned biblical Christianity. Fundamental doctrines have been set aside while New Age teachings are promulgated with impunity. Some churches advertise New Age programs and seminars, making no attempt to hide their apostasy. New Age teachings, Eastern religions as well as liberation, feminist and process theologies have become the chart and compass to set the liberal church's new course.

New meanings cloak old vocabulary. People in the pews hear familiar words, but most are blind to the fact that the words have been given new meanings. Denominational materials endeavor to persuade church members that it is appropriate to question the authority of the Bible and to adopt a new code of morality. "Times have changed," they tell them, "and so must you." Liberal church leaders subtly indoctrinate the laity into believing that the Bible no longer means what it says. Instead, it means what they say it means. Sin, repentance and salvation are no longer part of the liberal church's proclamation. Sadly, there are congregations where the people in the pews never hear biblical preaching of law and gospel. Some church members do not have even a memory of an authentic salvation message.

The ordination of women into the sacred office of the ministry has resulted in unbelievable changes within mainline churches. Feminists are rewriting Scripture, liturgy and theology. They have changed the name of God the Father to God the Mother. Some radical feminists have introduced pagan goddesses through their teachings in order to project what they call the feminine aspects of deity. Unable to believe in the God of the Bible the feminists and their supporters have created deities in their own image. This is not an aberration; it is an organized effort involving the cooperation of many denominations, including the World Council of Churches and the National Council of Churches.

THE ATTACK AGAINST THE CHURCH

The ecumenical movement has always been a bloody battlefield in the war for the church. Liberal clergy in the past habitually compromised the faith through cooperative efforts with the World Council of Churches and the National Council of Churches. However, their compromises pale when compared with present church leaders, including evangelicals, who are joining with pagan religions, cults and sects to form a one-world religion. The Parliament of World Religions and Thanksgiving Square are but two of many organizations which have prostituted the church on the altars of pagan gods. There are literally hundreds of organizations which are networked together to develop and promote the New World Order and the one-world religion. These organizations are led by Christian clergy and laity, world-religion leaders, pagan priests and priestesses, and even witches. Such alarming facts should concern every true believer regarding the future of the church and America.

Mega-denominations have become masters in the art of wresting authority from local congregations. Church bodies afflicted with merger-mania have gobbled up one another until they achieved power to control the destinies of local congregations and pastors — property, pews, pensions and all. As denominational membership declines or as money is harder to come by, mergers are once again on the minds of church leaders, and the whole merger process begins again. The people in the

4

pews rarely hear what the leadership elite have planned for them until it is too late.

With each merger, local congregations are assured that the new church will be stronger and more effective. Bible-believing church bodies concerned over the prevailing liberalism among the merging groups are encouraged to participate in the merger where they can be "salt and light," helping to turn things around. However, there is not a single instance in modern history where a Bible-believing church body entered into a merger with liberal churches and was successful in turning things around. Instead, they were swallowed up by the larger and more liberal entities. Within a few years of a merger, nearly all Bible-believing churches become indistinguishable from their liberal counter-parts. The "salt and light" argument is hollow. It was used on conservative church bodies in order to prompt their participation in the World Council of Churches and the National Council of Churches, yet the apostasies of those organizations worsen with every passing year.

Control and power are the objectives of most denominations. In some church bodies it takes two congregational votes with a two-thirds plurality in order to withdraw from the denomination. Even then, some power-driven denominations require additional permission from church authorities. Such heavy-handedness often intimidates church members to keep silent rather than risk losing their property or dividing the congregation. The enemy is not always subtle, but he is always clever!

Membership in mainline churches is in serious decline, but their leaders haven't a clue as to what is causing the mass exodus. They walk around in a fog trying to figure out why so many are leaving. Periodically ad hoc committees are formed to investigate the problem of membership loss. Sometimes they offer seminars which promote programs designed to halt the hemorrhaging. However, the real answers seem to elude the denominational experts, and their contrived gimmicks work ever so briefly, if at all.

At the same time conservative churches are growing in unprecedented numbers. A coincidence? Hardly! People are leaving their liberal denominations in droves and uniting with Bible-believing churches because they are sick and tired of having the latest chapters of the social gospel rammed down their throats. These spiritual refugees, seeking to preserve their Christian heritage, look for Christ-centered worship experiences and for pastors who preach the Word of God without compromise.

5

The vast majority are not leaving liberal churches, however. Consequently, their souls and the souls of their children are in peril. They are continually bombarded by Bible-denying clergy with new scriptures, new liturgies, new theology, new morality and bizarre worship experiences. People in the pews are confused, especially when the new teachings and practices are presented by trusted pastors.

Most mainline church members remain uninformed regarding efforts to take control of their denomination. Many do not realize that their church body is rewriting the Bible and theology, or is linked with false religions. Some laity have handed over all theological matters to their church leaders, believing whatever they are told. As long as the church building and the pastor are there on Sunday mornings, they remain content. They do not understand that the denomination into which they were born and reared has been disconnected from the Lord.

THE ATTACK AGAINST BELIEVERS

Jesus asked his followers a most profound question, "... When the Son of Man cometh, shall he find faith on the earth?" (Luke 18:8). His prophetic and rhetorical question sheds light on the pitiful condition of the modern church where little is left of biblical, apostolic Christianity. Today orthodox Christianity is primarily found in conservative, Bible-believing denominations. The spiritual enclave of those who hold to biblical Christianity is rightly characterized as the "Remnant Church." Their faithfulness to the Word of God is often viewed with contempt by both the liberal church and society. Mainline church bodies have toleration for every religious group under the sun except for Bible-believing Christians.

Most people who have read the last book of the Bible know how the battle for the soul of the church will end — Jesus Christ and His true Church will gain the inevitable victory. This certain triumph, however, does not mean that Christians are free to stand by while the forces of evil produce havoc in the church. All true believers are called to perseverance and faithfulness until Jesus comes again.

ENGAGING THE ENEMY

Christians are wrong to close their eyes while millions are being led astray by false teachers and promoters of evil. Christians in conserva-

6

tive churches are especially wrong to think that the battle for the soul of the church does not concern them. Doctrinal and moral compromises can and do take place in Bible-believing churches. Vigilance is demanded. Many liberal churches were once Christ-centered, Bible-believing congregations. How can Christians in orthodox fellowships turn their backs on members of mainline denominations who are endeavoring to stand against these destructive forces? Concerned Christians certainly cannot ignore the millions who are being led down the path to eternal damnation. Believers are charged by the Lord to "... pull them out of the fire ..." (Jude 23).

Contending for the faith is not an option — it is a command. Contending for the faith is the natural response of an obedient heart to the Word of God. Contending for the faith does not mean that we are to be contentious, mean-spirited or unloving. It does not mean that we are to dwell on this theme and no other; that would warp our lives and mar our testimonies. It certainly does not give us license to attack people or to be judgmental in our attitudes.

Contending for the faith means that we focus on issues, upholding the clear teachings of the Word of God. It further means that we stand without compromise against the assaults of those who would water down or deny the basic fundamentals of the faith.

Our objective is to pass on a living faith to the generations that follow us. As believers, our response to false teachers and unbiblical practices must be based solely on the Word of God, not on our feelings or personal desires. We must be filled with and function in the power of the Spirit of God if we are to effectively contend for the faith. Love for God and love for people should bathe every thought and action. We must be certain that we are dressed in the full armor of God and undergirded with prayer. Since the joy of the Lord is our strength, joy should be evident in our lives no matter how fierce the battle. Above all, we should be humble in heart. Arrogance and pride have no place in the battle for truth, for we have nothing which we have not received except by the grace of God.

AM I A SOLDIER OF THE CROSS?

Am I a soldier of the Cross,
    a follower of the Lamb?
And shall I fear to own his cause
    or blush to speak his Name?

Must I be carried to the skies
    on flowery beds of ease,
While others fought to win the prize
    and sailed through bloody seas?

Are there no foes for me to face?
    Must I not stem the flood?
Is this vain world a friend to grace
    to help me on to God?

Sure I must fight, if I would reign —
    Increase my courage, Lord!
I'll bear the toil, endure the pain,
    supported by thy Word.

The saints, in all this glorious war,
    shall conquer, though they die;
They see the triumph from afar,
    by faith they bring it nigh.

When that illustrious day shall rise,
    and all thy armies shine
In robes of victory through the skies,
    the glory shall be thine.

Isaac Watts, 1674-1748

Chapter 2

Contending for the Faith — our Duty

Beloved, when I gave all diligence to write unto you of the common salvation, it was needful for me to write unto you, and exhort you that ye should earnestly contend for the faith which was once delivered unto the saints (Jude 3,4).

The desire to avoid conflict is natural. Most Christians prefer to worship or engage in ministry rather than to oppose false doctrines or some pernicious evil that is being perpetrated on the church or society. Soldiers of past wars would have rather remained in the comfort of their homes than to have fought a bloody war across the ocean, but the choice was not theirs to make. Duty called and they obeyed. Today we enjoy our cherished freedoms because of the sacrifices that men and women of the armed forces made on our behalf. As Christians we occupy blood-bought ground, purchased by Christ and kept for us by an army of faithful soldiers of the cross. We must never take their sacrifices for granted or fail to understand our own personal obligations to pass on a living faith to the next generation.

SATAN'S GREAT DECEPTION IN SOCIETY

For most Christians contending for the faith is filled with negative connotations. That is the devil's lie, and many are deceived. While sin and immorality are widely accepted by society, opposition to those forces is often viewed with disdain. For example, those who protest the invasion of pornography into their homes and neighborhoods are frequently rebuked with cries of "censorship" and "separation of church and state." In a society where values are turned upside down, the pornographer has become the hero while those who oppose his lascivious work are the villains. Displaying a nativity scene on public property is considered improper, but the National Endowment for the Arts uses federal taxes to promote "art" that ridicules Christianity, such as a crucifix immersed in a jar of urine. Senator Jessie Helms of North Carolina has been lambasted by the liberals for voicing objections to these outrageous works being funded with public monies, but the NEA has been praised for its boldness to fund art projects regardless of public reaction. People for the American Way and the American Civil Liberties Union are viewed by much of the public as guardians of free speech and the First Amendment, whereas the American Family Association is portrayed as a threat to democracy.

Pastor Donald Wildmon of the American Family Association deserves the admiration and gratitude of the entire nation for his efforts to fight pornography as well as to curb violence and immorality on American television. Instead, he is portrayed as an arch-villain by the liberal media and those who desire an open society. Wildmon's organization, operating out of Tupelo, Mississippi, keeps the heat on media moguls from Hollywood to New York by monitoring the pornography industry and television programming. *The American Family Association Journal* lauds programs and advertisers promoting positive values, and it urges a boycott of shows and sponsors which disregard morality and decency, as well as businesses selling pornography.[1] Television producers who are seeking to increase the level of sex and violence in their programming despise Wildmon, especially when they have to scramble to keep their sponsors. Donald Wildmon, though vilified by the world, continues to contend for the faith, undeterred by his opponents.

SATAN'S GREAT DECEPTION IN THE CHURCH

False teachings and unbiblical practices of every description regularly flow into the church, but those who oppose them are typically portrayed as reactionary and negative. Conservative Christians are commonly labeled by the liberal press and the radical left as anti-gay, anti-abortion, and anti-everything-else. Christians often buy into this satanic deception, viewing themselves as negative if they stand in opposition to something that is contrary to the Word of God.

The truth is — false doctrines are negative and so are the people who promote them. Pornography and those who produce it are negative. The entire abortion industry is negative, as are the pro-abortion and homosexual movements. These negative forces are destroying America. It is time for Christians to get the facts straight and stop believing Satan's lie. Upholding biblical values and standing against those who promote evil is a positive action which honors the Lord. Satan's distortion of this truth is one of his most effective and frequently used tactics to silence Christians and prevent us from attacking his strongholds.

IMPEDIMENTS TO CONTENDING FOR THE FAITH

It is apparent to the most casual observer that many professing Christians are not standing against the forces of evil, and that the efforts of other Christians leave much to be desired. I trust that my observations will not be interpreted as an attack on any segment of the Body of Christ. My purpose is to show how vulnerable Christians can be if the whole Word of God is not heeded, or if the Christian life is not lived out in proper balance.

Perhaps the greatest impediment to contending for the faith is the mistaken belief that individual Christians are powerless to halt the intrusions of evil in the church and society. Many see the inroads of sin but choose to throw up their hands or leave the battle to someone else. Countless victories have been won by Satan and his legions without a fight. This attitude of acquiescence flies in the face of the Bible's teachings concerning Christian discipleship. Jesus told His disciples that each one must "... take up his cross and follow me." He warned that those who bear His Name would incur the world's wrath. "If they have persecuted me," said Jesus, "they will also persecute you." The Bible summons all believers to "... put on the whole armor of God, that ye may be able to stand against the wiles of the devil" (Ephesians 6:11).

God will give victory to His people. The history of the church, down to and including modern times, is replete with illustrations of Christians who met the enemy head-on and triumphed. Even if we are unable to halt the enemy at some point, it is our duty to stand against him and uphold the witness of the Lord. Satan's victories in the church and nation are due, not to his military genius, but to compromising Christians who have failed to keep the faith. Christians are without excuse since the Lord gives believers power through His Word and Spirit to overcome Satan in every circumstance because "... greater is he that is in you, than he that is in the world" (1 John 4:4).

11

IMPEDIMENTS AMONG EVANGELICALS

There are evangelicals who hesitate to contend for the faith because they erroneously believe that it interferes with evangelizing the lost. The policy of ignoring sin in order to reach the sinner is unbiblical. The Apostle Paul was a champion at reaching the lost and opposing all that was contrary to the gospel. Paul understood that false teachings are obstacles to evangelism which must be exposed if people are to be set free. Many evangelicals need to learn that lesson. Eastern religions and New Age cults are growing in large numbers around the world. Many of their converts and teachers are members of the Christian church. The damage caused by false teachers in the church is beyond calculation. We dare not take it lightly. The bonds of false teachings can only be broken by the truth. Jesus said, "And ye shall know the truth, and the truth shall make you free" (John 8:32).

An increasing number of evangelicals seem inclined to compromise the truth of God's Word. Many have made expediency a virtue, maintaining that the end justifies the means. Worship in some evangelical churches today resembles a three-ring circus or a theater. Show business is often used to draw crowds and stimulate church growth. People are invited to come to Jesus in order that they may feel good about themselves. Sin and repentance are rarely mentioned. Seldom do these compromising evangelical leaders encourage their people to contend for the faith because they are too busy promoting budgets, buildings and programs.

Instead of contending for the faith, an increasing number of evangelicals have developed ill-advised alliances with false religions, liberal churches and questionable organizations, ignoring their denial of the Word of God or their involvement in unbiblical practices. The unifiying factor for many of these alliances is what is commonly opposed, rather than what is mutually believed. Worship services involving evangelicals and Bible-denying churches are commonplace. Some evangelicals see nothing wrong with participation in worship services that include representatives of pagan religions. After all, they claim, it gives opportunity for them to witness the gospel. In fact, their cooperation sends a message to the "watching world"[2] that the departures from biblical Christianity are not really important after all.

IMPEDIMENTS AMONG CHARISMATICS

The charismatic movement which developed in the 1960s and 1970s had a significant impact on many congregations that had been consumed by liberalism or dead orthodoxy. It is not my purpose here to dissect the theology of the renewal movement which has created no small controversy, but I firmly believe that charismatics must bear a degree of responsibility for the low spiritual state of the modern church.

Some charismatics seem to care little about the erroneous beliefs of those with whom they fellowship as long as they profess baptism in the Holy Spirit. This is a dangerous and unbiblical practice. Portions of the charismatic movement have taken part in the doctrinal slide of mainline churches through excessive compromises with those who promote false teachings and false practices. Charismatic leaders have endorsed and participated in ecumenical efforts that involved grievous doctrinal departures, including apostasies in the National Council of Churches and the World Council of Churches.

Though the Bible clearly teaches that the cosmic struggle against spiritual wickedness involves every believer, some charismatics seem to believe that contending for the faith is counterproductive to their quest for spiritual fulfillment. They resist opposing false doctrines because they are so caught up in feelings and experiences. Their subjective experiences are often disconnected from the Word of God. The Spirit of God never contradicts the Bible, nor does He lead anyone into actions which violate biblical principles. Charismatics who claim to have a special "word from God" that encourages their participation in apostate associations are clearly wrong.

Numerous charismatic congregations, pastors and laity have opposed false teachings and false practices within their denominations. When it became clear that those denominations would not yield to the sovereign Word of God, they withdrew rather than participate in the abominations. Other influential charismatic pastors and congregations have continued to operate within the bounds of apostate denominations, seemingly oblivious to their many violations of God's Word. People who look up to them as examples and for leadership feel justified in remaining in Bible-denying settings, even at the peril of their souls.

Rodney Lensch, a leader in the Lutheran renewal movement, has encouraged believers in the Evangelical Lutheran Church in America to separate themselves from the apostasy of that body.

In these last days true believers need to affiliate with churches where the Bible is honored as God's inerrant, authoritative Word,

13

where the Holy Spirit speaks prophetically concerning the times in which we live and where church discipline is practiced so that error and evil are not allowed to contaminate the fellowship of the saints.

I personally have heard people say, "I could never bring my unsaved friends and loved ones to my church. They would be misled or confused by what is preached." What a sad predicament! When the lost start to panic and reach out for help in the days ahead we need to be able to invite them to churches where the gospel is consistently preached in the power of the Holy Spirit. How else, pray tell, can we "occupy until the Lord comes!" (Luke 19:13).

When the Lord was preparing to judge Sodom for its iniquity, He called Lot and his family to come out (Genesis 19:12-17, 2 Peter 2:6-10). In 2 Timothy 3 Paul describes the apostate church of the last days and says to the true believers, "Have nothing to do with them!" When the visible church welcomes the world into its fellowship without requiring repentance and faith, the true believers are to "come out from among them and be separate" for "what fellowship can light have with darkness?" (2 Corinthians 6:14-17).

In my estimation God would have to sovereignly and simultaneously visit every bishop, bureaucrat and theologian (as He did Saul of Tarsus) for the Evangelical Lutheran Church in America to be turned around and be spiritually set right. Since God is omnipotent He can certainly do so. But He is apt not to. And any lay person, pastor or congregation who thinks they can singlehandedly accomplish this would be as foolish as someone trying to repel a tornado by spitting in the wind. Why spend all your time and energy fighting a losing battle when you could advance the kingdom more effectively in a different context?

What is the lesson here for end-time believers? These are days when Jesus' absolute Lordship over our lives is being tested. He may call us out of our homes, our jobs, our cities and even our churches — for our spiritual safety. At such a time we may struggle as did Lot's wife. But Lord, I don't want to leave my church. I'm too old to do it. I'm a pastor and I can't afford to lose my health insurance or tamper with my pension. What will my parents

14

think? In such a moment, "remember Lot's wife!" Do what the Lord tells, however great the pain and discomfort, because the spiritual survival of you and your family may depend upon it.[3]

IMPEDIMENTS AMONG FUNDAMENTALISTS

Fundamentalist Christians as a whole have been faithful in contending for the faith and teaching its importance in the Christian life. They have endured ridicule and persecution because of their stand for the Word of God and their opposition to evil. Fundamentalists were among the first to decry the compromises of those associated with the World Council of Churches and the National Council of Churches. They have been on the front lines of many battles involving vital issues that threaten our nation. However, there is a tendency among some fundamentalists to make contending for the faith the supreme Christian activity. They seem to relish the fight for its own sake and forget what they are fighting for. Often they demonstrate little joy or love in serving the Lord. Their stridency damages their credibility with many who otherwise might be won. While such attitudes are the exception rather than the rule, they tend to reflect on the entire fundamentalist community.

The most alarming stituation which has developed within a number of fundamentalist churches is that they no longer practice the doctrine of separation with consistency. Expediency and political considerations are elevated above biblical commands which forbid such alliances. Perhaps it is reflective of our times that even some fundamentalists are willing to compromise the Word of God for the sake of expediency.

IMPEDIMENTS AMONG LIBERALS

No portion of the church bears as much responsibility for the doctrinal and moral slide evidenced in Christianity in the present century than liberal denominations. It is obvious to the most casual observer that mainline churches are on the wrong side of most issues. Often they speak and act in contradictory terms. For example, several years ago the Minnesota Council of Churches joined member churches in opposing various forms of gambling in the state. Yet in 1993, the Minnesota Council of Churches accepted a gift of $500,000 from one of Minnesota's largest gambling organizations.[4]

There is no need to elaborate on the liberal church's countless impediments in contending for the faith, as much of this book is devoted to that topic. My concern here is directed to those members of liberal churches who love the Lord and desire to be obedient to His Word.

Within all liberal denominations, Christians will be found who stand in opposition to their denomination's unbiblical views and practices. Some are vocal, others are not. Many support the pro-life movement and other conservative causes. However, the greatest impediment among these conservative Christians who endeavor to contend for the faith is their association with a church body that endorses nearly everything that they oppose. Their witness is tainted from the beginning by their church's stand on moral and doctrinal issues. They must continually apologize for their denomination's unbiblical positions. Bible-believing members of liberal churches must expend their energies opposing sin in their own denomination rather than upholding moral values within society. These well-meaning believers financially support ministries that are dedicated to fighting sin and evil; yet they place their offerings in the plates of their congregations which are then used to support the very causes they oppose. They rarely comprehend this inconsistency.

Clearly, Christians in every part of the church are vulnerable to having their witness marred when they embrace concepts, beliefs and alliances that are not upheld in Holy Scripture. Our ideas, no matter how right they may seem, have no merit unless they are in accord with the Scriptures. The key questions for all believers involving every issue of life should be: 1) What does God's Word declare about this matter? and 2) How may I effectively witness truth to those around me without compromising the Word of God?

Satan attacked the early church from without through emperors and edicts. Later, he attacked the Body of Christ from within through popes, priests and false teachers. Satan found his greatest successes came when he used corrupted church leaders and compromising Christians. This is still his favorite tactic.

OCCUPY THE BLOOD-BOUGHT GROUND

It is not easy to stand for truth in today's pleasure-loving, Bible-denying world. But when has it ever been easy? The growing intoler-

16

ance of the liberal church and society for those who espouse biblical values is a serious and present threat. Faithfulness to the Lord may mean the confiscation of church property, the loss of employment, friendships or status in the community. Whatever the cost, Jesus commands us, "... be thou faithful unto death, and I will give thee a crown of life" (Revelation 2:10).

Every Christian is a soldier of the cross and part of the Church Militant. Being a soldier for Christ is who we are, not just something we do. It is our responsibility to stand with every fiber of our being against the enemy of men's souls and all that hinders the work of Christ. The Body of Christ can be revived as Christians live out the true faith in the love and power of the Holy Spirit. America can still be won for the Lord as we press on faithfully. Christ has promised that the gates of hell shall not prevail against the church. We have been commanded by the Lord of the Church to demolish Satan's strongholds, pretensions and arguments. Opposing Satan and his destructive work is an integral part of soul winning. It is positive. It is good. It is our duty. May we be faithful unto death, or until Jesus comes again.

ONE CHURCH, ONE FAITH, ONE LORD

Thy hand, O God, has guided thy flock
    from age to age;
The wondrous tale is written full clear
    on every page.
Our fathers owned thy goodness,
    and we their deeds record;
And both of this bear witness,
    One Church, one Faith, one Lord.

Through many a day of darkness,
    through many a scene of strife,
The faithful few fought bravely
    to guard the nation's life.
Their Gospel of Redemption —
    sin pardoned, man restored —
Was all in this enfolded,
    One Church, one Faith, one Lord.

And we, shall we be faithless?
    Shall hearts fail, hands hang down?
Shall we evade the conflict,
    and cast away our crown?
Not so; in God's deep counsels
    some better thing is stored;
We will maintain unflinching,
    One Church, one Faith, one Lord.

Thy mercy will not fail us,
    nor leave thy work undone;
With thy right hand to help us,
    the victory shall be won;
And then by men and angels
    Thy Name shall be adored,
And this shall be their anthem,
    One Church, one Faith, one Lord.

Edward Hayes Plumptre, 1821-1891

Chapter 3

Contending for the Faith — of our Fathers

And others had trial of cruel mockings and scourgings, yea, moreover of bonds and imprisonment: They were stoned, they were sawn asunder, were tempted, were slain with the sword; ... (of whom the world was not worthy:) (Hebrews 11:36-38).

The low spiritual state of the church today has its parallels in other periods of history. The lamp of truth had been nearly extinguished prior to the Reformation when the church was riddled with corruption and apostasy. The Roman Church joined forces with kings and governments to wipe out every vestige of protest and opposition. In a later epoch, Protestant churches also persecuted Christians who opposed them. Who can imagine the sorrow of God as He watched His blood-bought church move further away from "the faith which was once delivered unto the saints?" Yet God has never left His church without a witness, even in the darkest times. The Scriptures declare: "When the enemy shall come in like a flood, the spirit of the Lord shall lift up a standard against him" (Isaiah 59:19).

John Wyclif and John Hus stood their ground against a perverse and wicked generation more than 100 years before the Protestant Reformation. They both proclaimed biblical authority over papal authority. While their theologies were mingled with error and not fully evangelical, they used the understanding they had to bring the church back into the way of truth.

More than a century later came Luther, Calvin, Zwingli and Knox whose voices neither emperor nor pope could silence. These stalwart men wrestled the captive church from the hands of the enemy and rekindled the lamp of truth. A new day dawned for the Body of Christ when the Reformers restored the great biblical doctrines — grace alone, faith alone and Scripture alone.

Tyndale who masterfully translated the Bible into the English language was faithful unto death to the Word of God and the testimony of Jesus. The Wesleys dared to defy those who wanted to embalm and entomb the living Word of God and rob precious souls of salvation. Later Hauge, Finney, Spurgeon, Moody and Sunday brought fires of revival to churches around the world. A host of lesser known warriors of the cross also fought the enemy in the trenches so that we might possess the pure gospel of Christ. The effective labors of these and other faithful servants of God ought to be an encouragement to Christians in the present age to pray and work for renewal of the true faith. The same Spirit who empowered them is present today to lead the church to victory.

The following are brief historical summaries of four Christians whose faithful witness for the Lord cost them dearly. Their commitment, sacrifice and labor for the Kingdom of Christ make our own efforts seem small. We are humbled by so great a heritage of faith. The major Reformers are not included here only because so much has already been written about their lives and courageous acts.

JOHN WYCLIF

One hundred and forty years before the Protestant Reformation, John Wyclif, known as the *Morning Star of the Reformation*, challenged papal authority. Wyclif was born in Yorkshire, England around 1328. Educated at Oxford, Wyclif spent most of his life as a scholar and teacher in that institution. He was greatly influenced by the writings of Augustine, as was Luther. Through his study of Scripture, Wyclif began to question various teachings of the church, especially the authority of the papacy. A schism in the church at that time produced two popes, each claiming that the others should be damned. According to church historian Roland Bainton, Wyclif contended that both were right. It was not until the last 10 years of his life that Wyclif gained significant influence through his writings and preaching.

Scripture was paramount in Wyclif's theology. He wrote:

The Bible is the Word of God, it is the Book of Life, and every Christian should study it. Every syllable in the Bible is true, it is the whole truth we find in God's Word; and the duty of every priest is to make God's Word known to the people.[1]

Believing the Bible to be the ultimate authority for testing all doctrine, Wyclif condemned the cult of the saints, indulgences, relics, masses for the dead and transubstantiation. He was convinced that formal services could impede true worship. However, being a product of the educational system of his day Wyclif held on to some traditional teachings, including purgatory.

Wyclif's criticisms of corrupted clergy stirred the ire of church authorities, especially the Archbishop of Canterbury. He was summoned before the Council of Bishops at St. Paul's Cathedral in London in 1377, and questioned about his teachings. Wyclif's association with the influential Duke of Lancaster not only spared him from being declared a heretic, it also gave him new boldness to spread his teachings in England and Europe.

Wyclif had the Scriptures translated from the Vulgate into English, believing that common people were capable of understanding them. His own words will give ample evidence on this point: "We ought to believe in the authority of no man unless he say the Word of God. Believers should ascertain for themselves what are the true matters of their faith by having the Scriptures in a language which all may understand."[2] He organized and sent out itinerant evangelists to preach the gospel to the general population. The evangelists were instructed to "teach in the vernacular the Lord's Prayer, the Ten Commandments and the seven deadly sins." Many people were led to faith in Christ. Wyclif's followers and adherents became known as Lollards. Their influence was felt not only in England but also throughout central Europe and Bohemia where John Hus took up Wyclif's efforts to reform and restore the church.

The Parliament enacted laws against the Lollards in 1406, banned unlicensed preachers and condemned Wyclif's doctrines as well as his translation of the Bible. While Wyclif was never physically persecuted, many Lollards were imprisoned and burned at the stake. Ordinary people whose hearts had been captured by the gospel of Jesus Christ surrendered to the flames rather than recant their loyalty to the Word of God. One such martyr was a tailor named John Badby who was fastened to the stake with chains, and the wood placed around him was ignited. The Prince of Wales standing near the place of execution ordered that the flames be extinguished; then he offered the tailor his freedom if only he would submit to church authority. John Foxe in his famous *Book of English Martyrs* reports:

This valiant champion remained deaf to all the promises of the prince, being more possessed by the Spirit of God than by any earthly desire. He could be allured by no rewards, but as a valiant soldier of Christ continued steadfast until life had gone from him, standing quietly in the midst of the fierce flames they had kindled.[3]

Sir John Oldcastle, another Lollard, was put to death for his faith in 1414. Though friends with the King of England, Oldcastle was jailed in the Tower of London before he was "hung alive in chains and slowly burned by a fire kindled beneath his feet." [4]

Wyclif died of natural causes in 1384. In 1415, the Council of Constance posthumously condemned Wyclif on 260 counts of heretical teaching, ordered his writings burned, and his bones cast out of consecrated ground. Thirteen years later, the Pope ordered that the remains of Wyclif be dug up and burned, so fierce was the hatred against him. Though they repeatedly tried to punish Wyclif years after he was in his grave, they could not destroy the truth he proclaimed. The embers of his efforts to restore biblical authority to the church eventually ignited the fires of the Protestant Reformation.

JOHN HUS

John Hus, a priest and a scholar, was another early reformer who preceded Luther. As with Wyclif, his education and training made it difficult for him to fully apprehend the evangelical teachings of the Bible. However, his was a bright light in a dark world. John of Husinee, a small town in southern Bohemia, was born of humble parentage in 1369. His name was later shortened to John Hus. Educated at the University of Prague, Hus became dean of philosophy and rector of the University.

Hus was greatly influenced by Wyclif, having personally hand-copied many of his writings. He differed with Wyclif on several points, especially transubstantiation. He often preached in Latin, but preferred to preach in Czech which endeared him to the people. Hus believed the Bible to be the supreme authority in all matters of doctrine and that Christ, not Peter, was the foundation of the church. John Hus was especially adamant against the sale of papal indulgences, as would be Martin Luther 100 years later. His teachings eventually brought him into serious conflict with church authorities.

In 1410, the Pope ordered that the writings of John Hus be gathered and burned. Hus refused his demand, though several of his works were found and destroyed. His popularity with the Czech people and Bohemian political leaders allowed him to continue preaching and writing even though his works had been declared heretical. However, confrontation with church authorities was inevitable.

John Hus was summoned to appear before the Council of Constance in 1414. He had been promised safe conduct, but on arrival he was imprisoned in a dark and damp dungeon. His fate was sealed when the Council condemned the person and writings of John Wyclif, whose influence continued to cause them no end of difficulty. After months of imprisonment and many appearances before the Council, Hus was turned over to civil authorities to be burned at the stake. On July 6, 1415, Hus was led to his execution and given one last opportunity to recant, but he refused to capitulate. As the flames raced to consume him, his last words were, "Lord, into thy hands I commend my spirit."

Hus never believed that he had deviated from true doctrine. During his trial he stated:

> I trust that by God's grace I am a sincere Christian, not deviating from the faith. I would rather suffer the dire punishment of death than to put forth anything contrary to the faith or to transgress the commands of the Lord Jesus Christ. ... Hence I wish that the Fictor (Palec) would show me today one precept of sacred Scripture that I do not hold. ... And if I ever taught anything I should not have taught, I am ready humbly to revoke it. But I trust that I shall sooner appear before the tribunal of Christ before he finds me to deny one jot of the law of the Lord! [5]

The followers of John Hus, known as the Hussites, carried on his teachings after his death. Several decades later, a group of Hussites became known as the Bohemian Brethren. The Moravians also trace their beginnings to the Hussites. The influence of John Hus in the life of Luther and other Reformers was significant.

HANS NIELSEN HAUGE

History corroborates that the need for revival in the churches has existed throughout the ages. The Lutheran Church in Norway was no

23

exception. God sent Hans Nielsen Hauge, a humble farmer, to labor in fields of the Norwegian Lutheran Church that were overgrown with formalism and dead orthodoxy.

Hans Nielsen Hauge, born April 3, 1771, in Tune Parish, Norway, was reared in a devout home and nurtured in the Word of God. His conversion to Christ came at age 25, while he was working on his father's farm. That very day he led his sister Anna to the Lord, and a short while later he led his brothers and parents into a living relationship with the Savior.

Hans' mother questioned his sanity for a brief period following his conversion because he spoke with everyone he met concerning their relationship with Jesus Christ. The passion in his soul to win people to Christ soon caused close friends to wonder about his state of mind as well. Hauge struggled with God's will for his life, questioning why God should not send "a bishop or other high person to convert people." Out of that struggle came the sure conviction that, for whatever reason, the call of God to preach the gospel was upon him.

Hauge printed a little book in 1796 in which he said:

> I plead with you, as tears are streaming down my face, that you do not let the devil blind you and harden your heart. Don't be satisfied with a dead faith. I testify unto you that you will go to perdition unless you are wholeheartedly converted to God. It is only by a true and real conversion that a soul can obtain the living faith, be saved and bear fruit for God.[6]

In 1797 Hauge walked throughout Norway, sharing the gospel of Christ in homes and on the streets. Shortly before Christmas of that year, he was arrested by order of a parish pastor and thrown into prison. A law dating to 1741 had banned lay preaching in Norway. While in prison Hauge led several prisoners to Christ. Upon release he was ordered not to preach again.

Hans was arrested and imprisoned several times in 1798 and 1799 as he traveled about Norway. He used the time in prison to write books which were later published. After a lengthy imprisonment in Trondheim, Hauge walked 300 miles to his home in Tune Parish. People followed him along the way so that they might hear him talk about Christ. Revival broke out in one town, requiring Hauge to delay his homeward journey. Soon revival fires were burning across Norway, bringing no end of consternation to pastors in the State Church of Norway who referred to the revival as the Hauge movement.

Julius Bech, pastor of the Trondheim Cathedral, wrote a book against Hauge in response to the revival movement. Hans found the task of an itinerant preacher increasingly difficult as people were ordered by church officials not to give him lodging or food. Hauge crossed over to Denmark where he preached for awhile, but letters from Norwegian pastors were sent to Denmark to dissuade people from attending his meetings. After preaching several weeks in Denmark, Hauge returned to Norway where he was arrested again. This time his imprisonment was to last 10 years.

At his trial in 1804, Hauge was offered freedom if he would promise to stop preaching. He responded, "I cannot promise to discontinue my devotional meetings and my prayers, and I cannot see that these should be detrimental when so many gatherings are permitted where people carouse, get drunk and swear."

Hauge was first jailed in Hougsund, then transferred to an Oslo prison. His treatment in prison was severe, and conditions were cruel. He was permitted no books or writing material and no visitors. He lost his teeth and hair, and eventually his health weakened to the point of death. In the space of nine years, Hauge was subjected to 28 trials. He was set free December 23, 1814, broken in body, but not in spirit.

Friends helped Hauge purchase a farm just outside Oslo where he lived his last 10 years in very poor health. Though he was never able to publicly preach again, his house was continuously filled with people who wanted to hear him share the gospel. Even church officials visited him, having come to recognize his contribution to the church in Norway. In his last years Hauge continued to write Christian books and literature. Throughout his life he published 33 books, and over 250,000 copies in all were distributed. It is estimated that he walked over 10,000 miles to preach the gospel. Hans Nielsen Hauge died at age 53, on March 28, 1824. At the time of his death, lay-fellowship groups and prayer meetings had been organized in every one of Norway's 600 parishes. Hauge was buried in a cemetery near Oslo. On his tombstone is the following inscription:

Until his last breath he held fast to the faith, hope and love he had spread among others by word, deed, writings and Christian life. He lived in the Lord; he died in the Lord; by the grace of Jesus does he receive eternal salvation.

The influence of Hans Nielsen Hauge continues to this day in Norway and throughout the world. Norwegian immigrants to Europe and the United States faithfully witnessed the gospel, encouraging people to have a personal conversion to Christ and to live out their lives in holiness before God and man (Pietism). Many Lutheran congregations today highly esteem their Haugian heritage.

The Hauge Federation in the United States publishes a magazine, *The Morning Glory*, conducts spiritual-life seminars and sponsors tent-evangelism meetings.[7]

J. GRESHAM MACHEN

One of the first battles contesting the entrance of Modernism into mainline Protestant churches began in the 1920s in the Presbyterian Church in the U.S.A. Many Bible-believing Presbyterian pastors, including J. Gresham Machen, Carl McIntire and Francis Schaeffer, stood in opposition to those within their denomination who denied the inerrancy of Scripture and other foundational doctrines. The account of J. Gresham Machen's contending for the faith is most worthy of consideration.

Dr. Machen was born in Baltimore, Maryland, July 28, 1881. He graduated from Johns Hopkins University in 1901 and entered Princeton Theological Seminary, from which he received his B.D. degree in 1905. He studied for a year in Germany before returning to Princeton Seminary as an instructor in New Testament studies. His reputation as one of America's finest Bible scholars grew steadily. A masterful Greek scholar, Machen wrote several Greek textbooks which are still used today, even in liberal seminaries. This brilliant but humble professor subordinated his academic credentials to accept a role thrust upon him — contending for the faith in the Presbyterian Church in the U.S.A.

Speaking at the Moody Founder's Week Conference in 1924, Machen challenged his audience to stand for truth against a rising tide of Modernism. One year earlier, liberals in his denomination had adopted the Auburn Affirmation which set the church body on a course away from biblical truth. His comments to the gathering at Moody offer insights into his personal convictions and determination to stand against the assaults on the church:

> Paganism has made many efforts to disrupt the Christian faith, but never more insistent or insidious effort than it is making today. There are three possible attitudes which you may take in the present conflict. In the first place, you may stand for Christ. That is the best. In the second place, you may stand for anti-Christian Modernism. That is next best. In the third place, you may be neutral. That is perhaps worst of all. The worst sin today is to say that you agree with the Christian faith and believe in the Bible, but then make common cause with those who deny the basic facts of Christianity. Never was it more obviously true that he that is not with Christ is against Him.[8]

During his tenure at Princeton, Dr. Machen became increasingly alarmed by the inroads of liberalism in both Princeton Seminary and the Presbyterian Church in the U.S.A. In 1929, when he had exhausted all legitimate means to halt the rise of Modernism in Princeton, he helped to found Westminster Theological Seminary in Philadelphia where he became Professor of New Testament. Three other faculty members left Princeton Seminary that year to join Machen at the new Philadelphia seminary. Carl McIntire and Francis Schaeffer, students at Westminister Seminary during this period, would later affirm Machen's indelible influence on their lives and ministries. The teachings and writings of J. Gresham Machen are evident in the writings of both Schaeffer and McIntire, as in the following statement by Machen regarding liberals and the Bible:

> It is no wonder, then, that liberalism is totally different from Christianity, for the foundation is different. Christianity is founded upon the Bible. It bases upon the Bible both its thinking and its life. Liberalism on the other hand is founded upon the shifting emotions of sinful men.[9]

J. Gresham Machen protested vigorously as Modernists gained control of the Board of Foreign Missions in the Presbyterian Church in the U.S.A. His protests turned into action when graduates from Westminster Seminary were barred from serving in the denomination's mission fields because of their stand on the inerrancy of Scripture. Machen and those associated with him, having tried without success to reform the Board of Foreign Missions by bringing it into compliance with the Westminster Confession of Faith and the Holy Scriptures, founded the Independent Board for Presbyterian Foreign Missions. Machen served as the board's first president. This, along with his call for a boycott of synodical benevolences, brought him into confrontation with church officials. They ruled that anyone who was a member of the Presbyterian Church in the U.S.A. had to resign from the Independent Board for Presbyterian Foreign Missions. Machen refused to do so, claiming the order was a violation of the constitution of the Presbyterian Church in the U.S.A. Church officials brought him to trial in January 1935 and condemned him. Commenting on his trial, Machen said:

> I am condemned on the ground that I have disobeyed a lawful order, but not allowed to be heard when I offer to prove that the order is unlawful; condemned for making false assertions against the Board of Foreign Missions, but not allowed to be heard when I offer to prove that those assertions are true. It is difficult to see how ruthless unfairness could go much further than that.

> I cannot be a party to any such concealment ... I must, in fulfillment of my ordination pledge, do all I can to let light into this dark place. I shall be condemned by this commission for doing so. But I cannot regard it as any great disgrace to be condemned by a commission that has unanimously confirmed as its presiding officer a signer of a document, the Auburn Affirmation, that casts despite upon the holiest things of the Christian religion. This commission dishonored Christ before it dishonors me.[10]

In 1936, the General Assembly of the Presbyterian Church in the U.S.A., meeting in Syracuse, New York, defrocked J. Gresham Machen and Carl McIntire, who had stood with Machen against the Modernists within the denomination. At that time, McIntire, also a member of the Independent Board of Foreign Missions, was pastor of Collingswood Presbyterian Church, Collingswood, N.J. That same year Machen helped to found the Presbyterian Church in America. Edith Schaeffer commented,

> Dr. Machen had not begun by wanting to form a new church, but to reform from within, to "feed back" staunch, well-educated

Bible-believing pastors into the "old church" to stand against the wave of liberalism.[11]

A few months later while visiting several small churches in North Dakota, Machen developed pneumonia. He died January 1, 1937, at age 55.

The low spiritual life which existed in the church in past years was wondrously transformed through the faithful witness of Spirit-annointed Christians whose hearts were held captive to the Word of God. The same Spirit of God who prompted absolute devotion to the Word of God in the saints of the past is able to work His grace in our lives in these days of apostasy. We cannot achieve success in the battle to take back the church without total commitment to Christ. Armchair Christians will not get the job done. God's people must become engaged in the noble fight for truth and righteousness. Until and unless Christians are ready to offer themselves as a living sacrifice, the possibilities for revival and reformation within the Body of Christ remain remote.

PSALM 133

Behold, how good and how pleasant it is
for brethren to dwell together in unity!
It is like the precious ointment
upon the head,
that ran down upon the beard,
even Aaron's beard:
that went down to the skirts of his garments;
As the dew of Hermon,
and as the dew that descended
upon the mountains of Zion:
for there the Lord commanded the blessing,
even life for evermore.

Chapter 4

Contending for the Faith — not Denominational Distinctives

O Timothy, keep that which is committed to thy trust, avoiding profane and vain babblings, and oppositions of science falsely so called: Which some professing have erred concerning the faith (1 Timothy 6:20,21).

Timothy was a man of faith. His faith was passed down to him, first from his grandmother, Lois, and then from his mother, Eunice (2 Timothy 1:5). The women in Timothy's family witnessed the love and truth of Jesus Christ to him. Paul repeatedly instructed young Pastor Timothy to guard the spiritual heritage which had been entrusted to his care. That was to be accomplished in the power of the Holy Spirit (2 Timothy 1:14), and as Timothy studied the Scriptures so that he could "… rightly divide the Word of truth" (2 Timothy 2:15).

Timothy was further instructed to "preach the Word … with all longsuffering and doctrine," because Paul saw the day approaching "when they will not endure sound doctrine; but after their own lusts shall they heap to themselves teachers, having itching ears; And they shall turn away their ears from the truth, and shall be turned unto fables" (2 Timothy 4:2-4). That is surely an apt description of our own times.

The Holy Christian and Apostolic Faith handed down from one generation to the next is the complete revelation of God's Word, given by the divine inspiration of the Holy Spirit. It is like a precious jewel entrusted to our care. We have a responsibility to pass it on in its entirety and without flaw to our children and grandchildren. God intends that every home should be a depository of faith for the next generation. The disintegration of family life in America has taken its toll on future generations. The spiritual vitality of America's homes must be restored if we ever hope to see our nation returned to its biblical foundations. As Barbara B. Hart pleaded in her hymn:

O give us homes where Christ is Lord and Master,
  The Bible read, the precious hymns still sung;
Where prayer comes first in peace or in disaster,
  And praise is natural speech to every tongue;
Where mountains move before a faith that's vaster,
  And Christ sufficient is for old and young.

PERSONAL OPINIONS ARE NOT THE BATTLE GROUND

It is one thing to guard the faith of our fathers and mothers, it is another to become caught up in "profane and vain babblings and oppositions" (contradictions). The Greek word for "contradictions" is antithesis, referring to a completely opposite concept. It may also refer to opposing opinions or controversies.

Some Christians seem to delight in arguing fine points of doctrine for no particular purpose other than to be contentious. Others elevate their personal opinions to the status of church doctrine, offering little sympathy to those who disagree with them. Christians who cannot separate their personal opinions from biblical convictions are the most likely candidates to battle the brethren. Personal opinions that contradict biblical teachings usually evoke the strongest disagreements, and rightfully so. However, when the purpose of a discussion is to prove oneself right and the other person wrong, or when the discussion is not for the edification of the Body of Christ, it ought to be avoided if at all possible. As Christians, our goal is to win people to Jesus, not to win arguments. Engaging in "profane or vain babblings" or "contradictions" serves only to fracture the fellowship and damage Christian credibility with those outside the church.

The world loves to argue. That is evident in most of the talk shows on radio and television where people exchange their opinions and pool their ignorance in fruitless discussions. Absolutely nothing is gained when Christians debate spiritual matters with people of the world. Paul said, "The natural man receiveth not the things of the Spirit of God: for they are foolishness unto him: neither can he know them, because they are spiritually discerned" (1 Corinthians 2:14). Opportunities to witness the gospel of Christ are usually lost when Christians choose to argue over controversial issues. Being able to distinguish between biblical faith and human controversies is not always easy, especially when the two become blended. We must rely on the Word of God and the Holy Spirit to know when to speak and when to keep silent.

DENOMINATIONAL DISTINCTIVES ARE NOT THE BATTLE GROUND

Doctrinal differences within Christendom have abounded for centuries. Christians disagree in their interpretation of the Bible regarding Baptism, Holy Communion, baptism in the Holy Spirit, eternal security, the second coming of Christ, and the list goes on and on. These varied and often conflicting interpretations of Scripture are the reasons so many church bodies exist. While we politely refer to them as denominational distinctives, they are responsible for creating deep divisions within the church. For many Christians, denominational distinctives are what contending for the faith is all about. Thus, they spend their energies fighting one another, rather than fighting the enemy of men's souls. This focus on distinctives must change if we are to effectively contend for the faith. I am referring to honest differences of interpretation which exist among Bible-believing Christians, not to doctrinal differences where unbelief and twisting of Scripture are involved.

Most church members would "rather fight than switch" when it comes to their denominational beliefs. These distinctives are, after all, what make us Lutheran, Baptist, Presbyterian, Methodist or whatever else we may be. Unfortunately, we often identify church bodies and their members only by these distinctives. Baptists are people who baptize by immersion and believe in eternal security. Presbyterians believe in predestination. Lutherans baptize infants by sprinkling, believing that all children are stained with original sin from birth. Episcopalians place great stress on the Eucharist. The Assemblies of God believe in the baptism of the Holy Spirit as a second work of grace. All these statements are true but they do not represent the whole truth by any means.

Episcopalians who attend a Baptist church seldom feel comfortable with their informal atmosphere of worship. Methodists often become confused by all the liturgy in a Lutheran service. Non-denominational and independent churches cannot escape being identified with doctrinal distinctives and worship styles which both attract and repel. Between doctrinal differences and variations in worship patterns, Christians tend to stay on their side of the denominational tracks where they feel comfortable. With such deep feelings for their own denominations and so little tolerance for other theological views or worship styles, it is little wonder that many Christians often prefer to fight one another rather than the forces that are bent on destroying the true church and society.

According to the Scriptures, there is "One Lord, one faith, one baptism, One God and Father of all, who is above all, and through all, and in you all" (Ephesians 4:5-6). Deep down inside believers know there is only one correct interpretation of doctrine. Yet with a tinge of smugness or an overwhelming case of arrogance, some assume every jot and tittle of their denomination's interpretations of Scripture are correct, and all other church bodies will come to realize that some day.

Shortly after my book *The Church's Desperate Need for Revival* was published, I was criticized in a Lutheran publication because I quoted Charles Spurgeon, the great Baptist preacher of the last century. The writer stated that a Lutheran author should not quote anyone who is Calvinistic in his theology. Those who are ready to write off faithful servants of God simply because they do not belong to their own personal school of biblical interpretation need to examine their hearts in light of God's Word. When the battle for truth is raging, believers cannot afford to turn on one another.

THE LORD WILL CORRECT OUR VIEWS

A vast difference exists between error and false teaching. Error is usually unintentional, while false teaching is a deliberate attempt to go against the revealed Word of God. Jesus accused those who were enticing Christians to sin through idols and sexual immorality of false teaching, warning them of impending punishment if they did not repent. (Revelation 2:14). The disciples who wanted to impose circumcision and the law of Moses on Gentile converts were in error. They willingly accepted correction when the Word of God was opened to them (Acts 15).

Some Christians' views are so narrow, restrictive and intolerant that they practice their faith in isolation, refusing to recognize the validity of any other group or denomination if there is any point of doctrinal difference. One day the Lord of the Church will open the Scriptures for all believers as He did for the disciples on the road to Emmaus. He may charge us, as He did them, with being "slow of heart to believe," but He will show us clearly the true interpretation of all doctrines. It is possible that the first doctrinal correction which Jesus will set forth to His Church will not be the denominational distinctives that we cherished, but our lack of love and acceptance of all who were redeemed by His precious blood. On that day every mouth will be stopped, denominational distinctives will cease to exist, and the veil that had impaired spiritual vision will be removed. "What a day, glorious day, that will be!"

STANDING TOGETHER ON COMMON GROUND

Because there is but "one Lord, one faith, one baptism and one God and Father of us all," and because one day we will understand fully, we may rightly conclude that there is more to bind Bible-believing Christians together than there is to separate us. When our denominational distinctives are set aside, we discover how much common ground we share in basic beliefs. These fundamentals, with the exception of biblical inerrancy, are summed up in the Apostles', Nicene and Athanasian Creeds, concise doctrinal statements of the early Christian church. The Creeds were formulated to combat false teachings and to keep Christians walking in the truth.

For years the ecumenical movement has functioned not so much on common beliefs as it has on common unbeliefs. Their unified ability to deny fundamental doctrines has enabled them to operate in a broad arena where false teachings are both tolerated and promoted. In contrast, the Bible-believing church stands united in the fundamentals of the faith, which are grounded in the inerrant Word of God. We may disagree on fine points of doctrine; we may even disagree on major points of biblical interpretation, but we stand as one upon fundamental truths of the inerrant Word of God. These fundamentals include:

The divine inspiration of the Bible, the unchangeable and unalterable Word of God;

The sovereignty of the Triune God — Father, Son and Holy Spirit;

The creation of man and all things by the direct hand of God;

The incarnation and divinity of Christ, the only Savior of the world, who was born of the virgin Mary;

The vicarious and atoning death of Jesus Christ for the sins of mankind;

The bodily resurrection of Christ and His ascension into heaven;

The person and work of the Holy Spirit, the Lord and Giver of life, who awakens faith through the Word, who calls people to salvation by grace through faith in Jesus Christ alone, and who keeps them in the one true faith through His Word and gifts;

The promised bodily return of Christ to receive His Church unto Himself and to judge the living and the dead;

Everlasting salvation with Jesus Christ in heaven for the saved;

Everlasting damnation in hell with Satan and his hosts for the lost.

Protestant Christians also hold the three great Reformation principles as nonnegotiable truths — grace alone, faith alone and Scripture alone. Saints and martyrs fearlessly upheld the integrity of these doctrines to the death. These biblical teachings separate the true Church from cults and false religions.

Christians who believe the Bible is the inspired, infallible and inerrant Word of God have common ground upon which they can fellowship and labor. But when the absolute authority of Scripture is denied, there is no basis upon which to build Christian consensus. False teachers maintain that truth is relative, situational and evolving; no one is right; everyone is right in his own eyes. A believer who upholds the Word of God and whose heart is open to instruction by the Holy Spirit should be willing to surrender personal views for correct teaching from the Scriptures. However, one who denies the authority of the Word, relying instead on his own intellect, will go on from error to error. These persons will never be won by intellectual argument, but only by conversion to Jesus Christ and enlightenment by the Spirit of God.

The primary battle ground where we must "earnestly contend for the faith which was once delivered unto the saints" is found in these basic fundamentals. I do not have the answers to conflicting denominational distinctives. The Lord alone will solve that dilemma. But here and now, Bible-believing Christians have a responsibility to walk together in the truth of God's Word and hold to these basic foundational teachings that the whole church shares in common. We do not need to surrender our denominational distinctives to walk together in the faith; however, we do need to surrender our lack of love for Christians in other households of faith as well as our deeply rooted prejudices that they are somehow spiritually inferior to us.

True Christian doctrine is vital (1 Timothy 4:16). I do not for a moment suggest that we obviate or glibly pass over anything which is taught in the Scriptures, or that we compromise truth for the sake of unity as the liberals have done. There are church bodies and movements, even among those who profess belief in biblical inerrancy, that have twisted, distorted and glossed over basic doctrines. They need to be opposed as strongly as the most outrageous claims of the liberals. Whenever and wherever Christians can stand together for Christ against a common enemy, we must do so.

The assaults upon society today are not only coming against Lutherans, Baptists, Methodists, Presbyterians, etc., but also against every Christian family. Abortion, crime, drugs, gambling and pornography affect all Christians and should be opposed by all Christians. False teachers who promote immorality, deny the divinity of Jesus Christ, His bodily resurrection or other foundational doctrines should face the opposition of a united church.

Francis Schaeffer appealed for unity among Bible-believing Christians in his book *The Church Before the Watching World:*

> The real chasm is not between the Presbyterians and everybody else, or the Lutherans and everybody else, or the Anglicans and everybody else, or the Baptists and everybody else, etc. The real chasm is between those who have bowed to the living God and thus also to the verbal, propositional communication of God's Word, the Scriptures, and those who have not.

So in a day like ours, when the world is on fire, let us be careful to keep things in proper order. Let us find ways to show the world that while we maintain and do not minimize our distinctives, yet we who have bowed before God's verbalized, propositional communication — the Bible — and before the Christ of that Bible are brothers in Christ. This we must do in the face of liberal theology. We must practice an observable and real oneness — before God, before the elect angels, before the demonic hosts, before the watching liberals and before the watching world.[1]

BLEST BE THE TIE THAT BINDS

Jesus had stern words for the church in Ephesus (Revelation 2:4). The Christians there, once a thriving people whose hearts overflowed with a passion for the Lord and His Kingdom, had allowed the bonds of redeeming love to loosen and fall. While they continued to stand for truth and to oppose evil, their love for the Savior had diminished. It almost seems contradictory that the Ephesian church could be so stalwart in their stand for truth and yet be so lacking in their love. This is a vital lesson for us today. Love without truth or truth without love is equally unacceptable to the Lord.

In the early days of the church, pagans who observed Christians living out their faith were led to comment, "Behold how they love one another." The love of God within the Body of Christ not only binds us together, it attracts nonbelievers in this loveless world to desire what we have. One of the most effective weapons in our arsenal to break down the strongholds of the enemy is Spirit-given love.

If ever there was a time for the Redeemed of God to stand together, it is now. The nation, our families and Bible-believing churches are under attack as never before. This is the time for us to stand together in common purpose — to witness the saving gospel of Jesus Christ to a lost and dying world and to stand against all that opposes the Kingdom of God. True Christian unity is possible when our hearts are centered on the Person of Jesus Christ, and our wills are bound to the inerrant Word of God.

THE ATHANASIAN CREED

Whoever wishes to be saved must, above all else, hold the true Christian faith. Whoever does not keep it whole and undefiled will without doubt perish for eternity.

This is the true Christian faith, that we worship one God in three persons and three persons in one God without confusing the persons or dividing the divine substance.

For the Father is one person, the Son is another, and the Holy Spirit is still another, but there is one Godhead of the Father and of the Son and of the Holy Spirit, equal in glory and coequal in majesty.

What the Father is, that is the Son and that is the Holy Spirit: the Father is uncreated, the Son is uncreated, the Holy Spirit is uncreated; the Father is unlimited, the Son is unlimited, the Holy Spirit is unlimited; the Father is eternal, the Son is eternal, the Holy Spirit is eternal; and yet they are not three eternals but one eternal, just as there are not three who are uncreated and who are unlimited, but there is one who is uncreated and unlimited.

Likewise the Father is almighty, the Son is almighty, the Holy Spirit is almighty, and yet there are not three who are almighty but there is one who is almighty.

So the Father is God, the Son is God, the Holy Spirit is God, and yet they are not three Gods but one God.

So the Father is Lord, the Son is Lord, the Holy Spirit is Lord, and yet they are not three Lords but one Lord.

For just as we are compelled by Christian truth to acknowledge each person by himself to be God and Lord, so we are forbidden by the Christian religion to say that there are three Gods or three Lords.

The Father was neither made nor created, nor begotten by anybody.

The Son was not made or created, but was begotten by the Father.

The Holy Spirit was not made or created or begotten, but proceeds from the Father and the Son.

Accordingly there is one Father and not three Fathers, one Son and not three Sons, one Holy Spirit and not three Holy Spirits.

And among these three persons none is before or after another, none is greater or less than another, but all three persons are coequal and coeternal, and accordingly, as has been stated above, three persons are to be worshiped in one Godhead and one God is to be worshiped in three persons.

Whoever wishes to be saved must think thus about the Trinity.

It is also necessary for eternal salvation that one faithfully believe our Lord Jesus Christ became man, for this is the right faith, that we believe and confess that our Lord Jesus Christ, the Son of God, is at once God and man: he is God, begotten before all ages of the substance of the Father, and he is man, born in the world of the substance of his mother, perfect God and perfect man, with reasonable soul and human flesh, equal to the Father with respect to his Godhead and inferior to the Father with respect to his manhood.

Although he is God and man, he is not two Christs but one Christ: one, that is to say, not by changing the Godhead into flesh but by taking on the humanity into God, one, indeed, not by confusion of substance but by unity in one person.

For just as the reasonable soul and the flesh are one man, so God and man are one Christ, who suffered for our salvation, descended into hell, rose from the dead, ascended into heaven, is seated on the right hand of the Father, whence he shall come to judge the living and the dead.

At his coming all men shall rise with their bodies and give an account of their own deeds.

Those who have done good will enter eternal life, and those who have done evil will go into everlasting fire.

This is the true Christian faith. Unless a man believes this firmly and faithfully, he cannot be saved.

THE APOSTLES' CREED

I believe in God the Father almighty, maker of heaven and earth:

And in Jesus Christ, his only Son, our Lord: who was conceived by the Holy Spirit, born of the virgin Mary, suffered under Pontius Pilate, was crucified, dead, and buried: he descended into hell, the third day he rose from the dead, he ascended into heaven, and is seated on the right hand of God, the Father almighty, whence he shall come to judge the living and the dead.

I believe in the Holy Spirit, the holy Christian church, the communion of saints, the forgiveness of sins, the resurrection of the body, and the life everlasting. Amen.

THE NICENE CREED

I believe in one God, the Father almighty, maker of heaven and earth and of all things visible and invisible.

And in one Lord Jesus Christ, the only-begotten Son of God, begotten of the Father before all ages, God of God, Light of Light, very God of very God, begotten not made, being of one substance with the Father, through whom all things were made: who for us men and for our salvation came down from heaven, was incarnate by the Holy Spirit of the virgin Mary, and was made man: who for us, too, was crucified under Pontius Pilate, suffered, and was buried: the third day he rose according to the Scriptures, ascended into heaven and is seated on the right hand of the Father: he shall come again with glory to judge the living and the dead, and his kingdom shall have no end.

And in the Holy Spirit, the lord and giver of life, who proceeds from the Father and the Son: who together is worshiped and glorified: who spoke by the prophets.

I believe in one holy, Christian, and apostolic church. I acknowledge one Baptism for the remission of sins, and I look for the resurrection of the dead and the life of the age to come. Amen.

Chapter 5

Contending for the Faith — and the Word of God

All scripture is given by inspiration of God, and is profitable for doctrine, for reproof, for correction, for instruction in righteousness: that the man of God may be perfect, thoroughly furnished unto all good works (2 Timothy 3:16,17).

God has graciously gifted the church with His inspired, infallible and inerrant Word. Everything necessary for life and salvation is recorded in the Bible in flawless detail. Through the ages, Christians have drawn encouragement and solace from its unfailing promises in the hours of their deepest need. God's Word is forever settled in heaven. When the sun becomes a burned out cinder, God's Word shall still endure. When all the critics of Scripture are dead and buried, the Word which they have scorned will still live. There will be no doubters of God's Word on Judgment Day.

The historic doctrine of biblical inerrancy is not based on a flight to fantasy but upon incontrovertible evidence, internal and external. Archaeologists continue to confirm its reliability, even in the smallest details. Hundreds of fulfilled prophecies offer irrefutable evidence of Scripture's divine inspiration. Peter declared, "... that no prophecy of the scripture is of any private interpretation. For the prophecy came not in old time by the will of man: but holy men of God spake as they were moved by the Holy Ghost" (2 Peter 1:20, 21). Israel's restoration as a sovereign nation after nearly 2000 years of exile witnesses to the fact that God still honors His Word and fulfills His promises.

The Bible's critics may alter dates, argue over authorship, deny the miracles, distort the message, but the wildest critic has never suggested that any portion of the Old Testament was written later than 150 years before Christ. Yet hundreds of Old Testament prophecies relating to Christ's birth, life, death, resurrection and ascension were fulfilled to the last detail. The words of Peter are most appropriate:

43

Of which salvation the prophets have inquired and searched diligently, who prophesied of the grace that should come unto you: Searching what, or what manner of time the Spirit of Christ which was in them did signify, when it testified beforehand the sufferings of Christ, and the glory that should follow. Unto whom it was revealed, that not unto themselves, but unto us they did minister the things, which are now reported unto you by them that have preached the gospel unto you with the Holy Ghost sent down from heaven; which things the angels desire to look into (1 Peter 1:10-12).

JESUS' WITNESS OF SCRIPTURE

Jesus spoke often regarding the trustworthiness of Scripture: "… the scripture cannot be broken" (John 10:35); "Heaven and earth shall pass away, but my words shall not pass away" (Matthew 24:35); "Sanctify them through thy truth: thy word is truth" (John 17:17). Our Lord used the Scriptures to answer His critics and stand against Satan's temptations in the wilderness.

Jesus affirmed the existence of Noah, Daniel and Jonah as historic personalities. This flies in the face of those who claim that they were fabled characters from Old Testament lore. He called Daniel a prophet and quoted Daniel's prophecies about end-times. Jesus identified Moses as the author of the books ascribed to him: "For had ye believed Moses, ye would have believed me: for he wrote of me. But if ye believe not his writings, how shall ye believe my words?" (John 5:46,47).

When our Risen Savior encountered two disciples on the road to Emmaus the afternoon of His resurrection, He revealed Himself by "opening the Scriptures" to them. Isn't it amazing that Jesus did not identify Himself to them by simply showing His scars as proof of His physical resurrection? Instead, He presented to them the same source of evidence that you and I have available to us today — the Holy Scriptures. A short while later when the Lord appeared to the other disciples, He said, "… These are the words which I spake unto you, while I was yet with you, that all things must be fulfilled, which were written in the law of Moses, and in the prophets, and in the psalms, concerning me" (Luke 24:44).

MAINLINE CHURCHES CAST DOUBTS ON THE ACCURACY OF THE BIBLE

God's Word has been under attack every since Satan tempted Eve by asking her, "Did God really say?" The questions keep coming: Can we trust the Bible? Is its message true, or does the Bible contain myths, contradictions and fabrications? Is the Bible the Word of God, or does it only contain the Word of God? These are not rhetorical questions; they are being used by liberal theologians to cast doubts on the trustworthiness of the Scriptures.

Martin J. Heinecken, a Lutheran theologian, commented in his book *We Believe and Teach* :

> The Bible is, from one point of view, an altogether human book written by fallible human beings; yet God speaks through their words as they bear witness to him. It is not necessary, therefore, to regard every word in the Bible as accurate or absolutely correct in every sense. The Bible is not a textbook in geography or science or ordinary history. It is testimony literature and must be read as such throughout. The biblical writers were children of their times and were mistaken about many things about which we today may be better informed.[1]

The influence of those who deny biblical authority cannot be underestimated. Within the present century, the view that the Bible merely contains the Word of God has become the dominant position among most mainline churches. This low view of the Bible prevails in all liberal colleges and seminaries. The educational materials of these denominations routinely and matter-of-factly cast doubt on the accuracy of the Bible. The following statement in the *Search* curriculum of the Evangelical Lutheran Church in America is typical.

> Joshua and the battle of Jericho ... Many people are profoundly bothered by this story ... The story of the battle of Jericho is told in terms of religious ceremony ... Because of the liturgical casting of the narrative, it is very difficult to determine what it is that actually happened at Jericho. Did the event take place just as the chapter tells it, or (like many liturgical celebrations of the Christmas story) do we have to read between the lines to find out what actually happened?[2]

It is difficult to comprehend that so many churches have discarded fundamental doctrines in order to embrace false and often bizarre teachings. If only a few churches were promoting false teachings and immorality today, it would be serious, but not critical. However, entire denominations are producing educational materials in an attempt to influence church members to accept lifestyles and teachings which the Bible clearly condemns. Laity are being indoctrinated into a Bible-denying belief system based on the premise that just because it is in the Bible, "it ain't necessarily so." Liberals maintain that new insights unknown to the Bible writers make many Scriptures obsolete. They tell all who will listen that much of the Bible is based on myths and exaggerated accounts of historical events. Every day false teachers gain new converts and take their churches further down the road to spiritual ruin. Every doctrinal departure in the church, as well as every moral compromise in the nation, stems from the denial of biblical authority.

SPONG IS WRONG

Bishop John Shelby Spong, in his book *Rescuing the Bible from Fundamentalism,* devotes several pages to the proposition that the Apostle Paul's strong denunciation of homosexual behavior was due to the fact that he was a homosexual.[3] Spong, the Episcopal bishop of Newark, New Jersey, insists that Paul cannot be taken literally, because "he did not write the Word of God. He wrote the words of Paul. ..."[4] The bishop refers to Christmas and Easter as "ultimate truth and literal nonsense."[5] He further denies biblical morality, as well as the divinity, virgin birth and resurrection of Jesus Christ.[6]

Spong is wrong when he suggests that Jesus could never have understood Einstein's theory of relativity, and he is wrong when he claims the Bible teaches that the earth is flat.[7] There is nothing left of Christianity to believe for the bishop and those who agree with him. Bishop Spong's views are not an aberration; they are typical of liberal clergy in mainline churches who deny the basic doctrines of the Christian faith. Bible-believing Christians who are not alarmed over these attacks on biblical Christianity need to wake up and smell the fire and brimstone of God's judgment.

LITERALISM – THE LIBERAL'S STRAW MAN

Bishop Spong belittles those who believe in the inerrancy of Scripture by claiming that we always interpret everything in the Bible literally and with equal emphasis.[8] That is unadulterated balderdash! I do not know any conservative Bible scholar who approaches hermeneutics believing every verse of Scripture must be interpreted literally. Scholars who profess inerrancy know that portions of Leviticus, for example, relate only to Israel and had to do with the Israelites' tabernacle and ceremonial rituals. But in Leviticus, as in other portions of Scripture, the Bible presents a moral code with universal principles and laws for all peoples of all times, including the Ten Commandments that Spong declares are antiquated and no longer relevant.

When Jesus said, "I am the door," we know that He is not literally a door, but what He said is literally true, "No one comes to the Father except by me." Jesus' words were literally true, though He often used metaphors and figures of speech. The liberals' insistence that belief in inerrancy requires a literal interpretation of every verse is a straw man, designed to bolster their otherwise untenable position.

It is interesting to observe that while liberal theologians are sure that many accounts of Scripture are myths and fabrications, they freely quote Bible verses to suit their own purposes. They claim the right to determine what parts of the Bible are true and what parts are lies. Spong is certain, for example, that Jesus was not born of a virgin, He did not rise bodily from the dead, and He did not walk on the water. Yet he is absolutely sure that Jesus was born in Bethlehem, grew up in Nazareth and died in Jerusalem. How can he be certain of those facts? Are they not part of the same record that he has already determined to be flawed? The writer of the *Search* Bible study curriculum is convinced that there was a Jericho, a Joshua and a battle; he further believes there was a Bethlehem and a baby Jesus, but he cannot bring himself to conclude that other statements in those accounts are factual.

The same Bible that teaches there is a heaven also teaches there is a hell, but the liberals have stricken hell from the record because it does not fit the image of their "all-loving God." They seem unable to link God's holiness with God's love, as though these two attributes of God were incompatible. It is sin and God that are not compatible. The same God who loves sinners hates sin and will surely bring sinners to judgment if they will not repent and turn to Christ.

Mary Kraus, pastor of the Dumbarton United Methodist Church in Washington D.C., stated: "My congregation would be stunned to hear a sermon on hell." She said that her congregation views God as "compassionate and loving, not someone who's going to push them into eternal damnation."[9]

Liberals fondly quote Bible verses that uphold salvation by grace alone, and well they should, but they have no basis of support for any doctrine apart from the Word of God. They have created what one theologian calls "a canon within the canon," a "Word of God ... separated from the Scriptural text."[10] The logic of the liberals is flawed. Christians should not be deceived by their false accusations or their self-serving use of the Bible.

WHOSE BIBLE IS IT?

The National Council of Churches' *Inclusive Language Lectionary* states: "The Bible is the church's book — created by and for the church."[11] With that premise as a license, the NCC lectionary added to and took away from the sacred writings. For example, they changed the text of the Lord's Prayer to read, "Our Father and Mother ..." But is the Bible the church's book? Does the church have a right to change the text in order to accommodate modern views regarding theology and morality? Those who agree with the NCC premise that the Bible is a book written by men and owned by the church say "Yes." Those who believe what the Bible teaches — the Scriptures are God's inspired, infallible, inerrant and unalterable Word — offer up a resounding "No!"

There is no greater theological issue facing the church than biblical inerrancy. Everything rises and falls on this vital doctrine. J. I. Packer said:

> The church no more gave us the New Testament canon than Sir Isaac Newton gave us the force of gravity. God gave us gravity by His work of creation, and similarly He gave us the New Testament canon by inspiring the original books that make it up.[12]

The church is divided into two camps regarding the inspiration of the Bible. The first and oldest view maintains that the Bible is the very Word of God, written by men who were inspired by the Holy Spirit to pen its every word. This view represents the Bible's own teaching regarding biblical inspiration and authority.

A second view purports that the Bible contains or may contain the Word of God, but it is chiefly a book about God by men who wrote according to their own intellect and in the customs of their times. In the second view, "inspiration" is reserved only for certain thoughts or ideas, not the specific words themselves. Those who postulate the second view have brought every conceivable teaching into the church and passed it off as "newly inspired truth for our times." Every Protestant church body today is faced with this crisis regarding the truthfulness of Holy Scripture.

THE HISTORICAL-CRITICAL METHOD

Beginning in the last century and continuing to the present time, a large number of biblical scholars have written books and articles questioning the accuracy of the Scriptures. These scholars, convinced that the men who wrote the Bible were not necessarily given divine guidance, developed a system of biblical study known as the historical-critical method. Their system of study first appeared in seminaries and universities of Europe in the 19th century. Later it was brought to seminaries in the United States where it gained a slow but steady increase of adherents. Today nearly every mainline seminary teaches and applies the historical-critical method throughout its entire curriculum. The Roman Catholic Church officially recognized its validity in 1994. Every doctrine, including the resurrection of Jesus Christ, has been brought into question, mutilated or denied by scholars of this theological approach.

The word "critical" means "to critique" or "to examine." All Bible scholars, including conservatives, have employed what is known as textual criticism to examine biblical writings. This type of study has not purposed to question the authority of Scripture. Instead, textual scholars endeavor to determine the most accurate rendering of a particular passage according to the original language, using copies of the most ancient and reliable manuscripts available. Conversely, historical-critical scholars approach the biblical text with the premise that the Bible is a fallible book written by men whose writings were limited by their knowledge, times and culture.

Dr. Harold Lindsell, in his book *The Battle for the Bible,* presented a solid case for rejecting the historical-critical method and for affirming the church's long-held position of biblical inerrancy. Lindsell focused on mainline seminaries which sold out their historic positions on biblical inerrancy in order to embrace the historical-critical method. He quoted Dr. Walter Maier, the respected Lutheran Church-Missouri Synod preacher and scholar:

> Most of the scholars who use the historical-critical method base their analysis of the biblical text on certain rationalistic, anti-scriptural presuppositions, anti-supernaturalism, for example. They flatly reject the possibility of divine intervention and miraculous action in human affairs. They also operate with various arbitrary, unwarranted assumptions, such as the unreasonable bias that many accounts, which purport to, do not really present factual history. As a result, their interpretations often subvert the obvious meaning of clear Scripture passages, and the theological views they express often do not conform to the Word of God.[13]

Dr. Maier illustrated the thinking of historical-critical scholars as they approach the Bible.

1. When the New Testament evangelists composed their Gospels, they simply took over traditional short stories about Jesus which had been circulating in Palestinian Christian communities and worked these into running Gospel accounts. Practically all references to time and place ... are of the evangelists' invention and do not supply authentic information about the life of Jesus.

2. The miracles reported in the Gospels did not actually occur.

3. Many of the sayings attributed to Jesus were never spoken by him at all.

4. The Gospels contain many legends and myths, pure fabrications, which were given their form "in the interest of the cultus" and for purposes of education. Mythological and legendary material, which is the product of "pious fancy" and "active Christian imagination," is seen in the following Gospel accounts: the narrative of Jesus' baptism, the narrative of Christ's temptation in the wilderness, the transfiguration narrative, the narrative of the Last

Supper, the passion narrative, and the resurrection narrative. Liberal theologians regard it as one of the functions of form-critical investigation to help the twentieth-century reader to demythologize the New Testament Scriptures and early Christianity. Additional incredible and, indeed, blasphemous views arising from the modern, scholarly use of historical-critical methodology could be cited.[14]

One of the most influential scholars of the historical-critical school was Rudolf Bultmann. Today every scholar who seeks to demythologize the Scriptures has been influenced to some degree by Bultmann. Here are a few excerpts from his writings.

Many a word is attributed to him (Jesus) which he did not utter. ... One can only emphasize the uncertainty of our knowledge of the person and work of the historical Jesus and likewise of the origin of Christianity. The inner development of the life of Jesus was inferred from the development of his Messianic consciousness: that is, from his steadily advancing claim to Messiahship, of which he was not entirely certain at the beginning and accordingly kept secret, and which he publicly acknowledged only at the end of his life. ... Indeed, did he hold himself to be the Messiah at all, or was this the product of the faith of his followers?

Mark is indeed the oldest gospel, its narrative cannot be accepted as an exact account of the history of Jesus; that Mark is really dominated by the theology of the Church and by a dogmatic conception of Christ, ... his gospel is composed in accordance with his own ideas ... It is equally clear that the Resurrection narrative has been composed in the interest of faith and under the influence of devout imagination.[15]

What an amazing commentary that Bultmann is heralded in mainline Protestant seminaries as a great Bible scholar and his ideas are taught as truth.

Liberal Bible teachers today maintain that the first five books of the Bible were not written by Moses but by at least four authors which they identify as J, E, D and P. This theory has been taught to seminarians in nearly all mainline Protestant seminaries in recent decades. Marcus

R. Braun, a layman who faithfully contended for the faith in the Lutheran Church-Missouri Synod, described the efforts of a liberal scholar who espoused the J, E, D and P theory and subjected his research to a computer program that had been developed to test the accuracy of authorship. The multiple authorship of the Pentateuch theory was confirmed by the computer. However, the computer expert who developed the program decided as a matter of curiosity to run several of his own recently written essays through the J, E, D and P process. To his amazement, the computer informed him that three or more persons had written every one of his essays.[16]

THE BIBLE AND THE FEMINISTS

The Bible is too sexist for the feminists. They despise the Genesis account of creation, which teaches that Eve was made from a rib of Adam. They cringe at any suggestion that Eve first succumbed to temptation, then led her husband into sin. All male references to God are taboo for the feminists. They cannot tolerate the fact that the Savior, Jesus Christ, was male. Thus, they are rewriting and reinterpreting the Bible to make it conform to their anti-male views.

The National Council of Churches' non-sexist lectionary and their newly revised Revised Standard Version Bible are byproducts of the feminist movement. In the NCC's lectionary, Jesus cannot be called a king because that is a male term. He cannot be called the Son of God; instead, they refer to him as "the anointed one" or the "human one." An editorial in a liberal Lutheran publication sanctioned the National Council of Church's non-sexist lectionary, even if it meant sacrificing the accuracy of the text:

> The strength of this lectionary, for me, emerges in the very places where it has dared to go beyond literal translation. I don't know how to reconcile the innovations that I like so well with our need for accurate translation, but I think that in whatever future year we are finally ready for inclusive language Scriptures, we will also be ready to sacrifice a certain degree of literal accuracy.[17]

If the feminists understood the Scriptures, they would realize that God has revealed the names by which we are to address Him. The feminists need to understand how dangerous it is to trifle with either the Name or the Word of God. The Almighty left no doubt when He gave the Ten Commandments that His Name was to be held in deepest reverence. According to Psalm 138:2, God has exalted above all things His Name and His Word. Douglas R. Groothus, in his book *Unmasking the New Age,* appropriately comments on this point:

> The Bible doesn't avoid feminine images for God. Jesus likened God to a loving and saddened mother hen crying over the way-wardness of her children (Mt 23:37-39). God is also said to have "given birth" to Israel (Deut. 32:18). Yet God is never referred to as "she." The actions of God are sometimes described in feminine terms, but never is the person of God described as feminine. The Bible speaks of God the Father. Jesus taught his disciples to pray "Our Father who art in heaven, ..." God our mother is not mentioned.[18]

THE JESUS SEMINAR

The Jesus Seminar, composed of 70 liberal Bible scholars from mainline and evangelical denominations around the country, released their version of the gospels, *The Five Gospels: What Did Jesus Really Say?* The publication of their book came after years of study, debate and a bizarre voting process to determine which words in the Bible attributed to Jesus were actually said by Him. According to published reports, the Jesus Seminar scholars believe that 82 percent of what Jesus is reported to have said in the Bible is "only an approximation or an outright inaccurate telling of his sayings." According to these scholars, "the gospels were written by people in the early Christian church, with passages inserted or deleted to fit the context of debates of the day."[19]

The fifth gospel examined by the scholars and included in their book is the Gospel of Thomas, found in Egypt in 1945. The Jesus Seminar's gospels are color coded. Red is used to identify words which the scholars are quite certain Jesus uttered; gray is used for words that are questionable; and words which the scholars maintain Jesus never uttered are printed in black. Only the words "Our Father" are in red in their version of the Lord's Prayer. The Jesus Seminar scholars concluded that Jesus never taught the prayer to anyone.

One of the Jesus Seminar scholars is Dr. Arland Jacobson, a member of the clergy roster of the Evangelical Lutheran Church in America and a teacher at Concordia College in Moorhead, Minnesota. Dr. Jacobson stated: "People need to be reminded that whether Jesus said something or not does not touch the question of faith claims about Jesus as being true or not. The claims about Jesus Christ in the creeds are not based on his sayings or dependent upon them for their truth."[20] Yet the Bible clearly teaches that "... Christ died for our sins according to the scriptures; And that he was buried, and that he rose again the third day according to the scriptures ..." (1 Corinthians 15:3,4).

Jacobson, commenting on the criticisms of the Jesus Seminar, stated: "But it's the scholarship that is being taught in the seminaries to future ministers. It is not some far-out brand of scholarship that doesn't represent a pretty wide scholarly consensus."[21] That is one fact Jacobson got straight — the mainline church seminaries are teaching this apostasy to future pastors. Most mainline church members would be shocked if only they knew what their pastor believes (or denies) about the authenticity of the Bible.

Dr. Marcus J. Borg of Oregon State University and a member of the Jesus Seminar said:

> The picture presented of Jesus in the new book *(The Five Gospels: What Did Jesus Really Say?)* is of a social radical, a wise teacher, who makes observations on the passing scene in the form of short, pithy, memorable one-and-two-liners. We're making him more like a Buddhalike figure — not just another philosopher but a really big one.[22]

The Jesus Seminar scholars deny many doctrines relating to Jesus Christ, including His virgin birth, divinity, messianic stature, and His resurrection.

ALTERING SCRIPTURE, NO TRIFLING MATTER!

The Bible declares in 2 Timothy 3:16 that its words are inspired (God-breathed), though it was written by human authors (2 Peter 1:20,21). Proverbs states, "every Word of God is pure ..." (flawless), and warns against anyone adding to the revealed message (30:5,6). The same warning against adding to or taking away from the Scriptures is given by the Lord in Revelation 22:18 and 19:

> For I testify unto every man that heareth the words of the prophecy of this book, If any man shall add unto these things, God shall add unto him the plagues that are written in this book: And if any man shall take away from the words of the book of this prophecy, God shall take away his part out of the book of life, and out of the holy city, and from the things which are written in this book.

Adding to, taking away from, or changing the text of Scripture are very serious matters. It is my firm conviction that when true believers find themselves participating in a worship service or Bible study where liberties are being taken with the words of Scripture, they should protest vigorously and walk out if necessary. To be silent or to remain is compromise. We ought to be more concerned with pleasing God than with pleasing man.

LIFE AND POWER ATTEND THE WORD OF GOD

Whenever God's law and gospel are faithfully proclaimed, wonderful results are visible. During the period of the kings, Israel's spiritual decline became so severe that they lost the Scriptures. What an amazing commentary on the nation that was both the instrument and depository of God's written revelation to man. The missing scroll of God's Word was discovered as the temple was under restoration during the reign of King Josiah. The cry resounded throughout Jerusalem, "We have found the Book." Upon hearing the rediscovered words of Scripture, the king and his people repented in sack cloth and ashes. Revival ensued.

Today vast portions of the church, the depository of God's Word to man, have "lost the Book." Consider the revival which could descend upon the churches if God's Book was reclaimed and pastors would faithfully preach the Word. Imagine the changes which would occur in our nation if the pulpits thundered with God's Word regarding sin, repentance, morality and personal responsibility. Instead, the average congregation in the mainline church hears only the words of a watered-down, mutilated and compromised gospel.

THERE IS NO MIDDLE GROUND

People will not be saved because they profess faith in a flawless Bible. Salvation comes only to those who believe in Jesus Christ and His shed blood poured out for them at Calvary. But all we know of Jesus and the way of salvation is revealed in the Holy Scriptures. The acceptance of part of this revelation as inspired while holding the rest in question is not the work of the Holy Spirit. The Spirit both directs and enables us to believe all that God has revealed.

The time for fence-sitting is past. The time for eternal choices is now. Elijah's question on Mount Carmel needs to be heard today: "... How long halt ye between two opinions? if the Lord be God, follow him: but if Baal, then follow him ..." (1Kings 18:21). Palsied and lethargic Protestantism needs to be shaken to the core by the inescapable fact that we must choose between following God and His Word or following the prince of this world and his lies. There is no middle ground. "The Church of What's Happening Now" must be told that their false religion is about to be tested from on high. The people in the pews who are mesmerized by empty, unfulfilling "churchianity" must be confronted with the consuming fire of God's eternal Word.

Christians have a responsibility to oppose false teachers; and where their teachings are entrenched, Christians are directed to separate themselves from unbiblical positions in order that their testimony will not be marred and they will not become participants in evil (2 Corinthians 6:14-17). When confrontation with false teachings comes, there will be upheaval. If you think you can stand for the truth of God's Word today and remain popular, think again. False teachers and false prophets will not stand by in idleness while their sacred altars are under attack. Will we, like Elijah, stand courageous before the smirking, compromising forces of our day?

God help us to be faithful!

GOD'S WORD IS OUR GREAT HERITAGE

God's word is our great heritage,
   and shall be ours forever;

To spread its light from age to age,
   be this our chief endeavor;

Through life it guides our way,
   in death it is our stay;

Lord grant while time shall last,
   Thy Church may hold it fast

Throughout all generations.

Nikolai F.S.Grundtvig, 1783-1872

Chapter 6

Contending for the Faith —
Watchful for Subtle Deceptions

But evil men and seducers shall wax worse and worse, deceiving and being deceived. But continue thou in the things which thou hast learned and hast been assured of, knowing of whom thou hast learned them; And that from a child thou hast known the holy scriptures, which are able to make thee wise unto salvation through faith which is in Jesus Christ (2 Timothy 3:13-15).

Norman L. Geisler has said, "The Enemy does not waste time shooting shingles off the roof; he places dynamite at the foundation."[1] The psalmist asks, "If the foundations be destroyed, what can the righteous do?" (11:3). The foundational truths of God's Word are being attacked daily. Naive church members may view these attacks as doctrinal disputes or mere differences of opinion among theologians, but the future of Christianity and the survival of our nation are at stake. The spiritual bankruptcy of major denominations and the moral decay in society are proof of what happens when the foundations are destroyed.

The church's rejection of biblical doctrines has had a direct bearing on our nation. Liberal religious and political leaders have joined hands to secularize America. The Supreme Court's decision in 1962 to ban prayer from public schools has proven to be a watershed event in U.S. history. Eleven years later, the Roe v. Wade decision hastened the downward spiral of our American culture. Other court decisions and legislation which sanctioned sin have made clear that God is being shut out of public life. The United States of America, no longer secure beneath the banner of God's blessing or protection, seems oblivious to impending judgment.

Removing God from public life is one thing, removing God from the church is quite another. However, this is precisely what liberal clergy, feminists and New Agers are endeavoring to accomplish. Correct biblical doctrines are not just something to believe, they are the very foundation upon which we stand as a church and a nation. Debates in church conventions regarding God's truth were not the harmless exercises many were led to believe. The pitiful state of the American church did not just happen; it was produced through one doctrinal compromise after another. Some church bodies may have passed the point of no return on the road to judgment because of their denial of the faith, as well as their sanction of evil and idolatry. The Lord has declared, "... My spirit shall not always strive with man ..." (Genesis 6:3). God's warnings to rebellious and idolatrous Israel finally were exhausted:

> And the Lord God of their fathers sent to them by his messengers ... because he had compassion on his people, and on his dwelling place: But they mocked the messengers of God, and despised his words, and misused his prophets, until the wrath of the Lord arose against his people, till there was no remedy (2 Chronicles 36:15,16).

We pray that America and her churches will repent and turn back to God before it is too late.

CHRISTIANS IN DENIAL

Many Christians are in denial when it comes to doctrinal and moral departures within the church. The most typical response seems to be, "Well, it's not happening in my denomination; it's all those liberal Methodists, Presbyterians and Lutherans." When false teachings within their denomination become obvious, people console themselves by observing, "Those things are happening in California, Minnesota or New York; they don't concern us here." Confronted with heresy and apostasy in their local area, church members often say, "But my pastor doesn't believe that; he preaches good sermons." Finally, when doctrinal departures are undeniably in their own congregations, the stubborn of heart exclaim, "At least I don't have to believe that way." Christians must wake up! A doctrinal departure or a false teacher in any part of the church sooner or later affects us all. As the church goes, so goes the nation; as denominations go, so goes the local congregation.

KEEPING FOCUSED ON PRIMARY ISSUES

Christians who are shocked over their denomination's efforts to sanction sexual immorality have every right to be alarmed. However, as serious as the sexual issues confronting the churches may be, there are doctrinal issues that are far more ominous because they threaten the very essence of Christianity. Most members of liberal churches have no conception regarding the impoverished spiritual condition of their denomination, or of the plans devised by radical leaders to reconstitute Christianity into a humanistic faith.

It is not possible in one book to expose all the assaults on foundational doctrines being devised today, but we will consider several of the more subtle deceptions that will have lasting implications if they should be successful.

THE SUBTLETY OF DECEPTION

The most astute student of the Bible may have difficulty discerning the subtle message of false teachers today. Even theologians are not always able to filter the vocabulary of those whose intent is to deceive. Religious words are used, but their meanings are not remotely connected with biblical definitions. Unaware that familiar spiritual expressions have been redefined by deceptive teachers, people in the pews function under a false sense of security as they are being indoctrinated into a revised version of Christianity. Without knowing the full meaning of what they hear, church people are easy prey for deceivers.

In certain church settings, unsuspecting laity are taken on a "spiritual journey" where God's "feminine side" is presented, or where they can get in touch with themselves. All the words seem so right — prayer, meditation, holiness, spiritual awakening and love. Feelings of inner peace and spiritual excitement are stirred through cleverly devised exercises. People become convinced that their warm feelings and new insights are caused by divine illumination, forgetting the Bible's warnings that some illuminations come from demonic sources:

> For such are false apostles, deceitful workers, transforming themselves into the apostles of Christ. And no marvel; for Satan himself is transformed into an angel of light. Therefore it is no great thing if his ministers also be transformed as the ministers of

righteousness; whose end shall be according to their works (2 Corinthians 11:13-15).

A few false teachers tend to be more obvious about their rejections of biblical doctrines. Theologians, such as Bishop Spong, are extremely open about their denials of fundamental truths. However, they are the exceptions. Today we have religious leaders who deny the need for personal salvation on one hand, but speak of spirituality and a living faith on the other. They deny that the Bible is the authoritative Word of God, but they constantly quote it to uphold their false teachings. Their rhetoric and writings contain just enough orthodoxy to confuse and confound most church-goers.

Liberation theologians love to quote John 3:16, "For God so loved the world ...," but that is where they stop reading. The world for them is forests, air, oceans and governmental systems, not people with souls that will perish unless they repent and turn to Christ. Their mission is to destroy capitalism and establish socialism. Most missionaries sent out by liberal churches no longer labor to convert people to Christ; instead they offer only humanitarian aid and affirm the lost in their pagan religions. When mission offerings are collected back home, people in the pews are given the impression that their contributions will be used to win a lost world to Christ. More deception!

THE NEW SPIRITUALITY

One of the most deceptive teachings today goes by the innocuous name of "Christian spirituality." What Bible-believing Christian, upon hearing that expression, would not initially be drawn to embrace it? After all, every true believer wants to be led by the Spirit of God. However, this inclusive theology with its orthodox name is a syncretistic mix of Christianity, New Age and Eastern religions. It is being taught in mainline colleges, seminaries, and churches as a continuation of historic Christianity, but in fact, it is heresy. Nothing offends teachers of Christian spirituality more than being linked with the New Age, but that is precisely what Christian spirituality is about.

Proponents of Christian spirituality frequently quote Scriptures, speak of salvation and Jesus Christ, as well as other Christian concepts. At the same time, they encourage their followers to participate in meditation exercises, taking "spiritual journeys" with "soul friends" and "spiritual directors." Bradley P. Holt, Professor of Religion at Augsburg College (ELCA), has written a book on Christian spirituality in which he states, "Christian spirituality is historical and global. It is an array of twenty centuries of development. It involves global connections with others whose cultures are very different from ours in North America."[2]

Holt's book *Thirsty For God, A Brief History of Christian Spirituality* uses inclusive language and quotes from the feminist-inspired New Revised Standard Version Scriptures. At the end of each chapter, Holt suggests exercises for persons seeking a closer relationship with God. One exercise, involving "The Jesus Prayer and Icons," directs participants to repeatedly pray the words "Lord Jesus have mercy on me." He warns readers not to hyperventilate during the exercise. Holt maintains that icons provide a "right brain" approach to prayer. Participants are further instructed to select and use an icon to commune with another person.[3]

Suggested readings in Holt's book include *Companions for the Journey Series, Praying with ... Hildegard of Bingen, Catherine of Sienna, Julian of Norwich,* etc., all favorites of the feminist theologians.[4] Those who endorse Holt's book on Christian spirituality include William A. Dyrness, Dean of the School of Theology at Fuller Theological Seminary; Mary R. Schramm, Manager of Martin's Table; Merton Strommen, founder of the Augsburg Youth and Family Institute; Timothy Lull, Academic Dean and Professor of Systematic Theology at Pacific Lutheran Theological Seminary; and Roberta Hestenes, President and Professor of Christian Spirituality at Eastern College (American Baptist).[5] Roberta Hestenes calls herself an evangelical Christian feminist.

George Lindbeck, Pitkin Professor of Historical Theology at Yale University, endorsed Holt's book with the comments:

> The questions and suggested exercises at the end of each chapter add to the usefulness as a text. In short, this is a uniquely appealing multicultural and non-Eurocentric initiation into the study of not only Christian spirituality, but post-biblical Christianity.[6]

Lindbeck's use of the words "post biblical" to describe the Christian spirituality movement is more accurate than he may realize.

Bradley Holt offers words of praise for New Age and former Roman Catholic priest Matthew Fox, "Fox's spirituality has many features that are attractive to me."[7] Holt also lauds liberation theology and believes the Week of Prayer for Christian Unity, sponsored by the World Council of Churches and the Vatican, illustrates the essence of Christian spirituality.

Christian spirituality organizations exist in mainline churches throughout the country. They are extremely popular in the Roman Catholic Church. Though advocates of Christian spirituality recoil when identified with the New Age movement, they claim that Christians can learn much from the spirituality of Native Americans, Hindus and Buddhists. In addition to Matthew Fox, those associated with Christian spirituality frequently quote Thomas Merton, Henri Nouwen, Richard Foster and a host of New Age writers, and they recommend their books.

Matthew Fox promotes his unorthodox view of Christianity with abandon. His books are not only lauded by the Christian spirituality movement, but also by the New Age, globalist and homosexual communities. Fox states:

> For while the Good News is that the Kingdom/Queendom of God has begun, the bad news is that it has not fully begun and is never fully incarnated — much less institutionalized — in any one form or expression of spirituality. The Holy Spirit will not be locked in to any one form of religious faith.[8]

> Unlike Fall and Redemption theology, which is dominant today, Creation spirituality is not patriarchal, but is feminist. It believes ecstasy, eros, and passion are not curses but blessings. Creation spirituality emphasizes beauty, not self-denial. It believes compassion, justice and celebration are the goals of spirituality. It emphasizes creativity over obedience. It believes humans are essentially divine.[9]

Matthew Fox heads the Institute for Culture and Creation-Centered Spirituality. Miriam Starhawk, feminist, witch, high priestess and a dominant figure in the New Age movement, is associated with Fox at the Institute. Starhawk regularly lectures at gatherings of mainline churches, even though her teachings are pagan and anti-Christian. The feminists in the church especially appreciate her goddess teachings and rituals. Fox, who was defrocked by the Dominican order because he refused to leave his Institute in Oakland, California and move to Chicago, joined the Episcopal Church.

Thomas Merton, a Roman Catholic Trappist monk, became involved with the Buddhist and Hindu traditions before his death and openly associated with the New Age movement. Holt stated that Merton "... stands as a witness for the contemplative life as a genuine Christian calling, without any 'social utility'."[10] Merton addressed the first World Spiritual Summit Conference in 1968, sponsored by the Temple of Understanding. He told the world religion representatives:

> Not that we have discovered a new unity. We discovered an older unity. My dear brothers, we are already one. But we imagine that we are not. And what we have to recover is our original unity. What we have to be is what we are.[11]

Two months later while traveling in Bangkok, Thailand, Merton touched an electric fan wire, killing him instantly.

Richard Foster, whose books are sold in Christian bookstores across the nation, has brought many New Age concepts into the evangelical community, such as *visualization* and the *inward journey*. In his book *Celebration of Discipline,* Foster stated:

> We of the new age can risk going against the tide. Let us with abandon relish the fantasy games of children. Let's see visions and dream dreams. Let's play, sing, laugh. The imagination can release a flood of ideas ... Only those who are insecure about their own maturity will fear such a delightful form of celebration.[12]

Foster's visualization concepts are often employed in evangelical churches as authentic expressions of Christian growth. The fact that much of Foster's writings are biblically sound seems to confuse some evangelicals, causing them to accept his non-biblical concepts as well.

Dave Hunt and T.A. McMahon offer a probing analysis of Foster's visualization techniques in their book *The Seduction of Christianity.* They quote a most revealing passage from Foster's book *Celebration of Discipline:*

> In your imagination allow your spiritual body, shining with light, to rise out of your physical body. Look back so that you can see yourself ... and reassure your body that you will return momentarily ... Go deeper and deeper into outer space until there is nothing except the warm presence of the eternal Creator. Rest in his presence. Listen quietly ... [to] any instruction given.[13]

Hunt and McMahon observed: "The Dalai Lama once stated, 'the use of the imagination to generate or visualize an image in the mind's eye' is an integral part of tantric Yoga; and he explained how this ancient practice is related to similar techniques recently adopted in modern psychotherapy."[14] They also commented:

> Christian leaders who promote and defend visualization seem unwilling to admit that it lies at the heart of religious beliefs that are demonically inspired and unalterably hostile to Christianity. They suggest instead that shamanistic visualization is a counterfeit of God's truth that they teach. However, there is no true visualization taught or practiced in the Bible for Satan to counterfeit; visualization is as absent from Scripture as it has always been present in the occult. Neither Isaiah, Jeremiah, nor any other biblical prophet created his visions through visualization, but received them by *inspiration* from God. Jesus didn't teach that His disciples could get Him to appear at will by visualizing Him, or that we should visualize what we are praying for. Yet this is taught by Christian leaders today who without intending to lead anyone into occultism are, nevertheless, pointing them in that direction by some of the methodologies they promote.[15]

Many congregations, evangelicals included, seem to think they cannot operate effectively without a gimmick to gain the attention of people in our secular society. They apparently believe a different approach must be acquired than the church down the street is using. At times, one wonders if there are any churches that still subscribe to unaltered, biblical Christianity. The program has yet to be devised that can compare with the Spirit-anointed preaching of God's law and gospel. Christian programs, seminars and curricula pose no danger in and of themselves. The danger comes when mortals think they can add something to the Word of God which will make it more palatable or more effective, or when they superimpose human works over facets of the Christian life which are produced by grace through faith alone, such as prayer.

When the disciples went to Jesus and requested, "Lord, teach us to pray," He did not tell them to engage in Yoga-like exercises, droning on with vain repetitions. He told them plainly, "... pray ye: Our Father which art in heaven, ..." Jesus also taught them, "But when ye pray, use not vain repetitions, as the heathen do: for they think that they shall be heard for their much speaking" (Matthew 6:7). Pastors who want to lead their people into a greater prayer life should close their New Age-inspired books and open the Holy Bible. The idea that Christians need to borrow anything from another religion to attain a higher spirituality should be an anathema to every true believer. God's Word is complete and fully adequate for humanity's every need. Christ-centered and biblically based materials, programs or activities are a blessing to the church; those that are not should be summarily rejected by God's people.

SUBTLE DECEPTIONS REGARDING SCRIPTURE

The doctrinal departure that should give Christians the greatest cause for alarm is the denial of the Bible as the inspired, infallible and inerrant Word of God, a subject covered in the previous chapter. After removing the authority of the Bible from consideration, or after casting doubt on its truthfulness, false teachers feel free to assault biblical teachings at will.

Paul told the Christians living in Galatia, "But though we, or an angel from heaven preach any other gospel unto you than that which we have preached unto you, let him be accursed" (Galatians 1:8). Those are strong words, but Paul understood the damage caused by those who twist and pervert the Word of God. Every doctrinal compromise in the history of the church can be traced to a toleration of false teachers, especially those who denied the absolute authority of the Holy Scriptures.

Today there are subtle teachings that lead people in the pews to believe their church leaders stand on the Scriptures to the last detail, when in fact, they do not. Wanting church members to think that they attach great importance to the Scriptures, liberal clergy speak about the Bible's value and urge their people to make Bible study a priority. However, they also claim the Bible is out of date when it comes to determining social values.

Herbert W. Chilstrom, Bishop of the Evangelical Lutheran Church in America, wrote an article entitled "Make Bible study a priority, You must come to your own Spirit-guided conclusions."[16] In his article, the Bishop sought to demonstrate the ELCA's support of the Scriptures by quoting from their "Statement of Faith." However, when the ELCA was formed, the words "inerrant" and "infallible" were deliberately excluded from their Statement of Faith. These two words which describe the inspiration and authority of the Bible were part of an "unalterable article" in the constitution of the American Lutheran Church, one of the bodies which now comprises the Evangelical Lutheran Church in America. The Bishop mentioned the word "inerrant" in his article, but only to show how unnecessary it is if a person's faith is centered in Jesus Christ instead of the Bible.

The ELCA bishop explained that Jesus Christ, the living Word of God, is the center of the Scriptures. He further stated that the chief purpose of the Bible is to bring us to faith and trust in Christ, not to be used as a rule book or a club, "or as a proof-text to substantiate everything we think about every imaginable subject." His statements undercut the authority of the Word of God by maintaining that we can find faith and life in Jesus Christ apart from the Scriptures. However, Jesus Christ and Scripture cannot be separated without doing violence to the doctrines of the written Word of God and the incarnate Word of God. Bishop Chilstrom stated:

> The Bible's purpose is to lead us to that place where we commit ourselves without reservation to Jesus Christ as our Lord and Savior. We are free. ... If we are grounded in the same faith, committed to the same Lord, we can allow for differences of opinion on matters that are not central to the faith.[17]

What the Bishop has written in the above statement is true insofar as it goes, but freedom in Christ is not a license to elevate one's opinions above the Word of God on any issue. The ELCA has repeatedly substituted its opinions for the Word of God through various statements and actions. The declaration by Bishop Chilstrom and other liberal theologians that Jesus Christ is the center of the Christian faith is correct, but not apart from the Scriptures. It is the Christ of the Bible who is central and authoritative to our faith. Even New Age teachers speak of Jesus Christ, but their christ is not the Christ of the Scriptures.

What is not readily understood when the Bishop claims that "we can allow for differences of opinion on matters that are not central to the faith" is the fact that he does not view inerrancy and infallibility of the Scriptures as essential. But, faith in Christ is not an ethereal concept. Faith in Christ is generated by the Holy Spirit through the Word of God. "So then faith cometh by hearing, and hearing by the Word of God" (Romans 10:17).

Bishop Chilstrom concluded his article by saying,

After careful study of the Bible, sincere brothers and sisters in the ELCA may come to different conclusions regarding such issues as war, human sexuality, the death penalty, abortion and other questions. Each of us must study the Bible, using the best resources available to us, and come to our own Spirit-guided conclusions. Not every believer will come to the same opinion. These differences need not divide us so long as we are held together by what is at the center — our conviction that Jesus Christ is the Son of God, our Savior.[18]

The "sincere brothers and sisters in the ELCA," mentioned by the Bishop, most certainly include homosexuals, lesbians, feminists, pro-abortionists, and theologians who have denied many fundamental doctrines. Those whose focus is on Jesus Christ as Son of God, apart from the absolute authority of the inerrant Word of God, will, indeed, come to many varied conclusions, including the ordination of homosexuals and the blessing of homosexual unions.

Studying the Bible and "using the best resources available," such as the ELCA's study on human sexuality, are not likely to produce a "Spirit-guided" conclusion. The Holy Spirit will not reveal anything that is contrary to the Word of God; therefore, the Holy Spirit and the Word of God cannot produce "different conclusions" to truth. Even though church members disagree on abortion, it does not alter the fact that God's Word forthrightly condemns killing unborn children. Individuals may conclude that homosexuality is an acceptable, alternate lifestyle, but even its endorsements by church conventions cannot obviate God's description of homosexuality as "an abomination."

So much of the world is in the church today, leading many to believe that one opinion is as good as the next, or that God's Word must be subjected to modern considerations. But Jesus Christ is "... the same yesterday, and today, and for ever, ..." (Hebrews 12:8) and His Words "... shall not pass away" (Matthew 24:35).

OTHER DECEPTIVE TEACHINGS

Deceptive teachings in the church are legion. Nothing is sacred to those who are determined to undermine the Word of God. Deceivers recite the Christmas narrative, but deny the virgin birth and the incarnation. Some false teachers tell of Jesus' miracles, then explain what "tricks" were employed to accomplish them. Others speak of Jesus' death on the cross, then deny His atonement for the sins of the world. Some say Christ died for all, but they interpret that to mean universal salvation, regardless of faith and belief in the Son of God. Some preach and write about the resurrection of Christ, while denying He rose bodily from the grave. Christ is coming again, the deceivers say, but His coming is spiritual, not literal. There is no end to the deceptions devised by the Deceiver himself. His success rate in our time is alarming.

SUBJECT TEACHERS AND PASTORS TO EXAMINATION

No loving parent would ever lace their family's food with poison, yet that is precisely what children and youth are receiving spiritually from the pulpits and classrooms of liberal churches. How can the average man or woman in the pew be discerning with the flood of theological "new speak" being thrust upon them today? Ask your teachers and pastors what they believe! Especially inquire about the beliefs of those who are teaching your children. Bible-believing pastors and teachers will not be offended if you ask about the basis of their beliefs. Those who have nothing to hide will be delighted that you cared enough to inquire. Teachers who are trying to re-educate the church with new doctrines and concepts will likely hedge and try to deceive. But be like the Bereans who listened intently to Paul and Silas, then "...searched the scriptures daily, whether those things were so" (Acts 17:11).

REGARDING SCRIPTURE

It is imperative that Christians uphold the Scriptures as the inspired, infallible and inerrant Word of God. You do not need to be skilled in theology to make an inquiry regarding the inerrancy of the Bible. Simply ask preachers or teachers if they affirm the doctrine of biblical inerrancy. They may respond, "O yes, I believe the Bible is inspired," but the word "inspired" can mean many things when it stands alone.

Press on with your inquiry. Ask specifically if they believe the Bible is without error and fully authoritative in all it states. If you encounter pastors or teachers who refuse to affirm the Bible as the inerrant Word of God, run, don't walk, to the nearest exit. Do not sit under their teaching no matter how "nice" they may be. All teachings and teachers must be subjected to the authority of the Word of God for the spiritual stability of your family and yourself.

REGARDING FUNDAMENTAL DOCTRINES

As a parish pastor I have always been concerned for the youth of my congregation, especially regarding the assaults their faith will sustain in their formative years. Every day there seems to be a new cult or sect seeking converts. Students are bombarded in public schools with humanism and New Age lies. Informing young people of all the dangers of the enemy is an impossible task. However, if young people are established on the solid foundation of biblical truth, they will be able, with the help of the Holy Spirit, to recognize the truth from the lie in every circumstance. Congregations need to place great emphasis on providing foundational instruction for children and youth.

The need for a solid foundation also applies to adults. Christians who are grounded in the Scriptures, who understand the plan of salvation by grace through faith in Jesus Christ alone, who know the truths affirmed in the Apostles Creed and the Ten Commandments, will not be easy marks for spiritual predators. When false teachers twist and distort the Word of God, or when they devise new methods to turn hearts, their deceptions will be seen for what they are, regardless of how they are packaged.

EXAMINE YOURSELF

My heart-cry is for every reader of this book to have a saving knowledge of Jesus Christ as Lord and Savior. As Paul said, "That I may know him, and the power of his resurrection, ..." (Philippians 3:10). A knowledge of correct doctrines, as important as they are, will not save; though false doctrines can and do destroy faith. Every person who is not born from above is both deceived and a deceiver. However, the Bible offers wonderful news:

If we confess our sins, he is faithful and just to forgive us our sins, and to cleanse us from all unrighteousness. If we say that we have not sinned, we make him a liar, and his word is not in us (1 John 1:9,10).

Search me, O God, and know my heart: try me, and know my thoughts: And see if there be any wicked way in me, and lead me in the way everlasting (Psalm 139:23,24).

If you do not know for certain that you will enter heaven when you die, ask Jesus Christ to come into your life and save you. Repent of your sins and receive the free gift of God's grace poured out for you at Calvary by the only Savior of the world.

I lay my sins on Jesus, the spotless Lamb of God;
He bears them all, and frees us from the accursed load:
I bring my guilt to Jesus, to wash my crimson stains
White in His blood most precious, till not a stain remains.

Horatius Bonar

I AM MUCH AFRAID THAT SCHOOLS
WILL PROVE TO BE GREAT GATES OF HELL
UNLESS THEY DILIGENTLY LABOR
IN EXPLAINING THE HOLY SCRIPTURES,
ENGRAVING THEM IN THE HEARTS OF YOUTH.

I ADVISE NO ONE TO PLACE HIS CHILD
WHERE THE SCRIPTURES DO NOT
REIGN PARAMOUNT.
EVERY INSTITUTION IN WHICH
MEN ARE NOT INCREASINGLY OCCUPIED
WITH THE WORD OF GOD MUST
BECOME CORRUPT.

MARTIN LUTHER

Chapter 7

Contending for the Faith — and Biblical Morality

Woe unto them that call evil good, and good evil; that put darkness for light, and light for darkness; that put bitter for sweet, and sweet for bitter! (Isaiah 5:20).

But God forbid that I should glory, save in the cross of our Lord Jesus Christ, by whom the world is crucified unto me, and I unto the world (Galatians 6:14).

Sexual immorality is not new — not in society, or even in the church! Immoral and deviant sexual sins have plagued Christianity through the centuries. News accounts of pastors committing adultery, or church members engaged in extra-marital affairs could have been published in any century of church history. The early church which functioned in a pagan culture fought numerous battles over moral issues, but righteousness prevailed. Paul chastised the church in Corinth for tolerating sexual sins within its fellowship (1 Corinthians 5). Jesus upbraided the church in Pergamum for allowing the promotion of sexual sins, and warned them to repent (Revelation 2:14-16). What is new regarding sexual immorality in today's church and society is its massive acceptance and official sanction, as well as the absence of prophetic voices to sound the alarm.

America can no longer be characterized as a Christian nation. The modern church exists within a pagan culture, and the pagan culture exists within the church. Many denominations have replaced biblical standards with the standards of the world. There was a time, and not so long ago, when Christian influence guarded the nation's life through its strong commitment to biblical morality. Holiness of life and conversation were viewed as virtues within all branches of Christendom. The Judeo-Christian ethic formed the foundation for American law through the middle of the present century, and protected America's citizens from abortion, pornography, gambling, prostitution, homosexual acts and even adultery.

Vast portions of the church no longer look to God's Word for guidance on moral issues, but to psychiatrists, psychologists, sociologists and other self-acclaimed experts whose vocabulary does not include the word "sin." The authoritative declaration "Thus saith the Lord" has been replaced with the self-serving expression — "Well, this is what I think about that!" Liberal denominations which have endeavored to sanction their humanistic opinions of immorality by rewriting the Scriptures, drafting statements and passing resolutions at church conventions are only deceiving themselves. God does not suffer from delusions. You can bathe and perfume a pig, dress it in a Christian Dior gown, deck it with jewels and enter it in a Miss America contest, but because of its natural inclination to wallow in the mud, it will always come out looking and smelling like a pig. Church statements and policies that approve what God's Word condemns fare no better.

Church members who believe their toleration and promotion of evil are going unnoticed in heaven are deceived. Judgment will fall on the churches, and America too, if repentance is not forthcoming. These are not the ravings of some idealist, but declarations of the Word of God. "The wicked shall be turned into hell, and all the nations that forget God" (Psalm 9:17). Those who doubt God's resolve to judge sin need only look into the graves of fallen civilizations — Sodom, Babylon, Greece, Rome and Nazi Germany. The Apostles' Creed aptly expresses, "... He shall come to judge the living and the dead." In his first inaugural address, George Washington stated:

No people can be bound to acknowledge and adore the invisible hand which conducts the affairs of men more than the people of the United States. Every step by which we have advanced to the character of an independent nation seems to have been distinguished by some token of providential agency ... We ought to be no less persuaded that the propitious smiles of heaven cannot be expected on a nation that disregards the eternal rules of order and right, which heaven itself has ordained.[1]

The only voices left to warn our rebellious nation to turn back to God are those of Bible-believing Christians — and far too many are silent! The cosmic battle over moral values that is now raging will determine the ultimate destiny of America and her churches. There is so much for believers to do, and so little time left in which to do it.

THE BRAINWASHING OF CHURCH AND SOCIETY

Social planners have determined to re-educate the public, not only to tolerate immoral behavior, but to accept it as normal. The method of choice to achieve their objectives is language. Language has been used successfully as a brainwashing technique throughout the centuries by social engineers. They know that by changing common vocabulary, society will eventually accept concepts that were once rejected.

Mainline denominations, including some conservative evangelical bodies, are falling into line with the evolutionary social planners as their Scriptures, hymnals, liturgy, writing and speaking lexicons undergo major revisions to make them nonsexist and politically correct. Public school text books are being carefully written by globalists, homosexuals and liberal educators to promote the acceptance of the New World Order and all it represents.

The vocabulary articulated by reporters on news broadcasts and used by the publishing industry has been deliberately chosen to conform with newly established standards. Feminist, homosexuals and political groups inform the media of words that are and are not acceptable. Nearly every minority in the country, with the glaring exception of conservative Christianity, is accorded such consideration by the liberal media. For example, the media seldom identifies Christians as being "pro-life"; instead, they are labeled as being "anti-abortion." Members of the media rarely apply the term "left wing" to liberals, but they constantly attach the term "right wing" to conservatives. Bible-believing Christians are referred to as the "Christian Right," but when is the last time you heard of the "Christian Left"?

The word "baby" is never used in media coverage when referring to an unborn child who is about to undergo fatal surgery in an abortion clinic — the term of choice is "fetus." Abortion is defined as "the removal of fetal tissue," or the "termination of a pregnancy." However, if a woman delivers her child several weeks prematurely, news reporters tell how doctors are working to save the life of the baby. The public is being brainwashed to accept politically correct vocabulary and doesn't even realize it. Language modification takes time, but it is effectively changing, not only the way Americans speak, but also what we believe.

ACCEPTING HOMOSEXUALITY AS A VIRTUE

Only a few years ago, Christians who described homosexual behavior as an abomination were considered as upholding biblical morality. Today persons with such views are labeled — even from pulpits — as homophobic, bigots, intolerant, and hate-mongers. Righteousness has been turned inside out. The term "homosexual" has become a badge of honor for many in church and society. What was once unthinkable has become the order of the day — the ordination of homosexuals, the blessing of homosexual marriages, the adoption of children by homosexuals, and the recognition of homosexuals as a legitimate minority.

Practicing homosexuals frequently speak at church services and youth events, where they indoctrinate persons of all ages into the acceptance of their soul-damning lifestyle. Public school authorities offer forums and classes in which practicing homosexuals extol the virtues of sexual deviant behavior. Children in public schools, through studies such as "Heather Has Two Mommies" and "Daddy's Roommate," are being conditioned to accept as fact that homosexual and lesbian families are just as normal as families with mommies and daddies. Even television sitcoms endeavor to mold the minds of the American public by promoting aberrant sexual behavior and by ridiculing those who oppose it. Some corporations now advertise their products through commercials and ads that feature homosexuals in family settings. According to the *Wall Street Journal,* the Dayton-Hudson stores have introduced a line of greeting cards which may be exchanged between a homosexual and a heterosexual.[2]

THE MYTH OF HOMOSEXUAL NORMALCY

Liberal churches and the media are helping to deceive the public through their distorted images of the homosexual lifestyle. Accordingly, an uninformed public makes the naive assumption that homosexuals are paired with one another in life-long bonds of fidelity, when in fact most homosexuals engage in dangerous, promiscuous sexual practices. Not surprisingly, homosexuals and their supporters don't tell about gay bars and bath houses where homosexuals engage in unspeakable sexual acts with numerous partners. The public is not informed regarding the number of homosexuals who must be treated every year for gonorrhea, syphilis, genital herpes, venereal warts, scabies, viral hepatitis (types A, B, and Non-A/Non-B), intestinal parasites and, of course, AIDS. Most people are unaware of the high suicide rate among homosexuals, or the guilt and inner pain they endure because of their bondage to sexual deviancy.

Homosexual activists boast about the fact that the American Psychiatric Association no longer views homosexuality as an illness to be treated, but they do not tell that the APA has thousands of psychiatrists who disagree with that decision. Enrique T. Rueda, in his book *The Homosexual Network, Private Lives and Public Policy*, describes how the National Gay Task Force was instrumental in maneuvering the APA into its decision to declassify homosexuality as an illness:

> Ronald Bayer, an Associate for Policy Studies at the Hastings Center, Institute of Society, Ethics and the Life Sciences, has written a carefully researched study on the process by which homosexuality "lost" its character as an illness and "became" a way of life; we have drawn extensively from his study, *Homosexuality and American Psychiatry,* in this section.

> On December 15, 1973, the board of trustees of the American Psychiatric Association voted to declare homosexuality not an illness. This vote followed a year of political maneuvers engineered by the National Gay Task Force. This vote was not the result of scientific analysis after years of painstaking research. Neither was it a purely objective choice following the accumulation of incontrovertible data. The very fact that the vote was taken reveals the nature of the process involved, since the existence of an orthodoxy in itself contradicts the essence of science. Nevertheless, the board acted unanimously, theoretically in the name of some 25,000 American psychiatrists.

> The response to this vote was even more astonishing. The psychiatric defenders of the view that homosexuality is an illness demanded and obtained a mail referendum on the Question. The National Gay Task Force panicked at the prospect of the referendum. Under its leadership, a letter recommending approval of

the board's decision was mailed to the members of the APA. This letter was signed by all three candidates for the presidency of the APA, including Judd Marmor.

In Bayer's words: "The National Gay Task Force orchestrated the process of obtaining signed copies of the letter, purchased the necessary address labels from the American Psychiatric Association, and underwrote the full cost of the mailing. ... Though the NGTF played a central role in this effort, a decision was made not to indicate on the letter that it was written, at least in part, by the Gay Task Force, nor to reveal that its distribution was funded by contributions the Task Force had raised. Indeed, the letter gave every indication of having been conceived and mailed by those who signed it."

Some 10,000 psychiatrists voted on the referendum, almost 6,000 favoring the board's action. If it is considered that there are almost 25,000 psychiatrists, the affirmative vote constituted less than 25% of the total number of psychiatrists. Nevertheless, the board's action stood approved.

What most people do not know, however, is that such a decision has no scientific value, expressing merely the wishes of the homosexuals themselves.[3]

THE MYTH OF HOMOSEXUAL NUMBERS

For years homosexual activists have touted the Kinsey report, published over 40 years ago, which numbered the homosexual population in America at 10 percent or more. Now reports have been released disclosing that the Kinsey figures were deliberately skewed. New surveys conducted by the Guttmacher Institute and the University of Chicago reveal that no more than 1 to 2 percent of the population consider themselves to be homosexual.[4]

THE POLITICS OF HOMOSEXUALITY

The homosexual political lobby is growing more powerful every day. The average citizen underestimates the influence that the homosexual community exercises in the political arena. "Gay Pride Week," celebrated across the nation with parades and public acclaim, is the result of political pressure being applied to public officials. In various states and cities, homosexuals have succeeded in influencing legislation which identifies them as a minority, and makes any kind of "discrimination" against them illegal. In San Francisco, Minneapolis, New York and other major cities, many local politicians need the support of homosexuals to be elected or to remain in office. In numerous parts of the country, health benefits have been extended to the "spouse" of a gay or lesbian worker.

President Clinton deliberately courted the homosexual community during his election campaign and made "gay rights" one of the primary objectives of his administration. He appointed several homosexuals and homosexual activists to high positions in the government, and immediately set out to admit gays and lesbians to the armed forces. Clinton's efforts to allow homosexuals to serve in the military appeared to have been derailed for a time by severely watered-down amendments, but now the "don't ask, don't tell policy" is in force with more rights for homosexuals than the general public realizes.

Three powerful homosexual organizations — the National Gay Task Force, the Gay Rights National Lobby and the Universal Fellowship of Metropolitan Community Churches — lobby for the homosexual agenda in the halls of local, state and national governments. These organizations have access to the White House, as well as overwhelming influence with many members of Congress. Hundreds of homosexual organizations are networked for greater effectiveness, and they have strong support from feminist and liberal organizations as well.

Homosexuals are organized in all mainline denominations, as well as in most educational institutions across the country. The Metropolitan Community Church, which has observer status in the National Council of Churches, constantly presses for full membership in that body. There are homosexual teachers' organizations and a Gay Task Force for the American Library Association. The Gay Fathers Coalition and the Lesbian Mothers National Defense Fund promote the adoption and rearing of children by gays and lesbians. Gay organizations function among seminarians, pastors, nurses, medical doctors, psychologists, scientists and social workers. One of the most infamous homosexual organizations is NAMBLA, the North American Man/Boy Love Association. Their goals are stated as follows:

> The North American Man/Boy Love Association (NAMBLA) is an organization founded in response to the extreme oppression of men and boys involved in consensual sexual and other relationships with each other. Its membership is open to all individuals sympathetic to man/boy love in particular and sexual freedom in general. NAMBLA is strongly opposed to age of consent laws and other restrictions which deny adults and youth the full enjoyment of their bodies and control over their lives. NAMBLA's goal is to end the long-standing oppression of men and boys involved in any mutually consensual relationship by:
>
> 1) building a support network for such men and boys;
> 2) educating the public on the benevolent nature of man/ boy love;
> 3) aligning [sic] with the lesbians, gay and other movements for sexual liberation; and,
> 4) supporting the liberation of persons of all ages from sexual prejudice and oppression.[5]

The United Nations recently granted observer status to the International Lesbian and Gay Association on the UN Economic and Social Council. Some members of the UN were alarmed when they learned that the North American Man/Boy Love Association is affiliated with the ILGA.

THE AIDS MYTHS

AIDS is the first politically protected disease to ravage the world. Disinformation about AIDS has been circulated by government agencies which have been intimidated by the homosexual lobby. Inflated figures regarding the number of persons in the U.S. who are infected by the AIDS virus helped influence politicians to allocate more government money to fight AIDS than any other disease. An article in the *Lambda Report* stated:

> The first nationwide survey of HIV infection shows that between 300,000 and 1,000,000 Americans are HIV positive — considerably lower than previous government estimates. The survey by the

82

National Center for Health Statistics found that only 29 of 7,992 (0.36%) Americans sampled were HIV positive.

In addition, statistics from the U.S. Department of Health and Human Services, Centers for Disease Control and Prevention show that 90% of all full-blown AIDS cases are people who practiced intravenous drug use and/or homosexual behavior.[6]

A report by Dr. John Seale of the Royal Society of Medicine, published in the minutes of Great Britain's House of Commons in 1987, listed the following items of disinformation commonly furnished to the public:

1. People with AIDS are categorized as belonging to a small number of "risk groups" giving the false impression that the vast majority of people cannot get AIDS.

2. AIDS is portrayed as only a behavioural disease caused by sexual and narcotic misdemeanors. This implies that if anybody gets AIDS it is their own fault.

3. Emphasis on transmission of the virus during sexual intercourse, and education as a solution to the epidemic, implies that the disease will disappear with modified behaviour. This misses the point that as the epidemic explodes, infection by chance, nonsexual contact becomes ever more common.

4. By equating sodomy with sexual intercourse the impression is given that homosexuals have just been unlucky to get infected before heterosexuals. In reality homosexual activity has spread the virus through the population at a vastly greater speed than normal sexual intercourse could achieve.

5. The value of blood tests for diagnosis of AIDS virus infection is repeatedly denigrated by those who do not want them introduced compulsorily. In fact the blood test is an unusually reliable diagnostic tool.

6. The suffering of those with AIDS is highlighted while ignoring the suffering of those who will get AIDS in the future if appropriate steps are not taken to stop its spread.

7. The rights of those infected with the virus are stressed, while

the rights of the uninfected to be protected from infection with a lethal virus are ignored and glossed over. Protection of the life of its citizens is one of the major obligations of the State.

8. Misinformation is perpetuated by homosexuals actively obstructing the publication, in scientific or general press, of facts and conclusions which they want suppressed.[7]

Dr. Lorraine Day, M.D., in her compelling book *AIDS, What the Government Isn't Telling You,* has also revealed how essential information regarding the spread of AIDS has been distorted or kept from the public. Dr. Day, who served as a member of the AIDS Committee of San Francisco General Hospital and the University of California, San Francisco, refers to the AIDS disinformation as "AIDSpeak."[8] She came under intense criticism for her revelations regarding officially suppressed and deliberately skewed information about the AIDS virus. In her book, Dr. Day reported how doctors are free to test, without permission, for any disease known to man except the AIDS virus. She further stated that patients are not entitled to know if their physician or surgeon has the AIDS virus.[9]

The case of a Florida dentist who infected several of his patients with the AIDS virus was given little notoriety by the medical profession or the media. Every time a report was given, commentators hastened to explain how such infections are rare and should not alarm the public. Yet anyone who has been to a dentist in the last few years knows that latex gloves and masks, as well as new technologies for the sterilization of instruments and equipment, are the order of the day for dental clinics. Dr. Day quotes from a report by the Pasteur Institute in Paris, France, that says "the AIDS virus in saliva remains alive and infective on a dry surface at room temperature for as long as 7 days."[10]

According to official government reports, AIDS is not likely to be passed through routine household contact, yet several cases of sibling children passing the AIDS virus to one another have surfaced. Efforts were made to suppress this information for fear of the public's reaction.

Government policy regarding AIDS is often political and lacking in the public's interest. People with AIDS have been permitted to enter this country, though persons with lesser infectious diseases were denied entry. Safe-sex campaigns advocating the use of condoms are dangerously flawed. Condoms are anything but safe in stopping the AIDS virus, and government officials know it. The AIDS virus can pass through microscopic holes, and condoms are full of such holes. The word "blame" is not in the vocabulary of government health officials or homosexual activists when telling how the AIDS virus is passed from one person to another. Though 90 percent of all AIDS cases involve those who engaged in homosexual behavior or intravenous drug use, ads and commercials produced by the government caution heterosexuals to protect themselves when having sex. Perhaps they know that television images of homosexuals depicting their deviant sexual practices would not set well with the American public.

Neither public morals nor the battle against AIDS were well served by Joycelyn Elders, Clinton's Surgeon General, who called for the U.S. government to consider the legalization of drugs and the development of sex education for children as young as 2 years of age. United Methodists in Florida, who had asked Elders to address their annual conference in June 1994, requested that she not speak because of her controversial and unbiblical statements on various moral issues. Interestingly, Elders accepted an invitation to speak that same day to a Minnesota synodical convention of the Evangelical Lutheran Church in America.

In spite of all the money being poured into AIDS research, scientists are no closer to discovering a cure for the disease. Recently, several new strains of the AIDS virus have been discovered that are not detectable through present forms of blood testing. Researchers now maintain that "... the human immunodeficiency virus, which causes AIDS, also can cause cancer rather than simply make patients susceptible by weakening their immune system."[11] Until a cure or effective treatment for AIDS is discovered, preachers and politicians would do well to warn the public that fornicating and sexual deviant behavior are not only immoral; they can produce deadly consequences.

THE CHURCH AND
THE HOMOSEXUAL MOVEMENT

In 1983, I vigorously protested a statement issued by the Minnesota Council of Churches that both endorsed and promoted homosexuality as a valid lifestyle. I was shocked to learn that my own Lutheran church body was largely responsible for the contents of their statement. In a meeting with my synodical bishop, Herbert Chilstrom, I stated, "The day our church decides to ordain homosexuals is the day I leave." He responded, "Then you had better leave now, because we have been ordaining homosexuals for several years." A few days later, the Minneapolis *Star Tribune* began a series of articles confirming the Bishop's admission that homosexuals were being ordained by the church. One article stated:

> The 30-year old pastor in northern Minnesota is the first acknowledged homosexual to be ordained by the Minnesota Synod of the LCA, but only after he promised to remain celibate. That was a year ago. Today, he is often lonely. But he said, "The compromise doesn't bother me. Maybe some radicals would say I sold out. But at least I got my foot in the door. Who knows how much I'll be able to do 10 years from now."

> "He's very conscious of the fact that he is a pioneer and that the pattern he sets could be crucial for others who want to be more open about their sexual orientation," said Minnesota Synod Bishop Herbert Chilstrom.[12]

Regardless of those published reports and my own public statements concerning the church's policy of ordaining avowed homosexuals, most people refused to believe it. Today there are few doubters.

The United Church of Christ was the first denomination to ordain practicing homosexuals. Several denominations, including the Evangelical Lutheran Church in America, ordain only avowed homosexuals who promise to remain celibate. While the homosexual lobby is not fully satisfied with this limited policy, they accept it. They know if they keep up the pressure, practicing homosexuals will be ordained in most of the Protestant churches in the future.

Pressure to ordain practicing homosexuals is being keenly felt in California where Ross Merkel, pastor of St. Paul's Lutheran Church, Oakland, was defrocked by the Evangelical Lutheran Church in America after he announced that he is in a "committed" relationship with a homosexual. Merkel's congregation has retained him as pastor. The Sierra Pacific Synod voted in April 1994, to send a message to the ELCA that the synod is standing behind Merkel and his congregation. This marks the first time that an entire synod of the ELCA has endorsed practicing homosexuals in the ordained ministry. The Sierra Pacific

Synod includes more than 200 ELCA congregations and 83,000 baptized members in northern California and Nevada.[13]

Some Christians appear surprised by gay and lesbian efforts to win the church's approval for their lifestyle, but practicing homosexuals in the church have had the endorsement of denominational officials for years. Nearly two decades ago, homosexual organizations were regularly invited to distribute literature and promote their cause at synodical conventions of the Lutheran Church in America. Most church members are unaware that large sums of money have been handed out by liberal denominations to homosexual organizations.

In 1987, a Lutheran bishop described how he went into the home of a homosexual "couple" and used his *Occasional Services* book to conduct a "Blessing of a Dwelling" which "in some small but real way affirms them in the relationship and invokes God's blessing on their lives." The same bishop stated that pastors may be asked to conduct a service — "blessing deep, meaningful and lasting relationships between gay or lesbian people."[14] Similar blessings and marriage vows of homosexual couples have taken place with and without the approval of officials in many mainline churches, especially in the ELCA. Members of the Evangelical Lutheran Church in America should have been neither shocked nor surprised when their human sexuality task force recommended that the blessings of homosexuals become officially endorsed by the church body.

At their constituting convention in 1987, the Women of the Evangelical Lutheran Church in America issued a paper entitled "Embrace God's World" that offered dozens of ways for church members to show their support for gays and lesbians:

By acknowledging the anniversary of a gay/lesbian couple and remembering the partner upon illness or death of a spouse.

By allowing your children to establish friendships with gays and lesbians. Many such folk are nurturing, love children and have parental desires. Having a special "aunt" or "uncle" in your family has blessing for us all.

By inviting gay/lesbian couples to participate in Couples Clubs; giving them one set of offering envelopes; and having their picture taken together for the church's pictorial directory;

87

By using inclusive language in prayers, sermons or lessons or announcements; change "husband and wife" to "partners, lovers, spouse, couples, beloved, etc.";

By discussing the possibility of a Lesbian Circle.[15]

In 1988, Lutheran Social Services of Northern California produced a program on AIDS, entitled *Step by Step, Youth and AIDS*. The program, offered to youth in Lutheran congregations, was also funded and supported by the Wheat Ridge Foundation and the Evangelical Lutheran Church in America. One of its weekly activities suggested:

Activities should be designed to explore facts about AIDS, transmission, and prevention. You can support and assist youth choosing to refrain from sexual activity with others prior to marriage with compelling reasons for their decision. For youth choosing to be sexually active with others prior to marriage, you can provide the information and tools for safe sex. If safe sex is to be effective, it is important to help youth *experientially* move past issues of shame, fear and denial. Don't just mention the word "condom." That's not enough. Have condoms at each session. Demonstrate how they are used. Have youth unwrap them, touch them and even blow them up. Some educators suggest planning activities around condoms — i.e. a "water-condom" toss, or a scavenger hunt where the youth have to purchase as one of the required items a box of condoms from a local drug store. Experiment with activities that will work in your community. **Youth must be desensitized to condoms if they are to prove effective as safe sex tools.**[16]

The United Church of Christ produced a curriculum on AIDS prevention for children and adults. Their study gives third and fourth graders descriptions of intercourse, while fifth and sixth graders are told, "No one chooses her or his sexual orientation. Our individual sexual orientation is part of God's goodness in creating us as sexual persons."[17]

The Evangelical Lutheran Church in America published a course for youth entitled *Let Justice Roll Down Like Waters,* written by a lesbian who served on the task force for ELCA's failed human sexuality report. Leaders of the course are instructed to divide the youth into small groups to brainstorm slang expressions used to describe homosexuals.

They are told to "set the tone for the exercise by giving permission for all words to be voiced in this context, even though individual group members feel it would not be appropriate in polite conversation."[18]

RE-INTERPRETING WHAT THE BIBLE TEACHES ABOUT HOMOSEXUALITY

One of the methods employed by homosexual activists to secure the church's approval of their lifestyle is re-interpreting the Bible. They have taken every reference in the Scriptures relating to homosexuality and twisted its meaning to suit their purposes. The homosexuals have enlisted well-known theologians to lend credibility to their efforts to cast "new light" on the Bible's teachings about sodomy. Their distorted interpretations of the Bible, lacking in scholarship and contrary to the apostolic Christian faith, are presented as fact in books and other literature, at Sunday schools, seminars, and forums. The homosexual activists' interpretations of the Bible may be the greatest distortions of truth ever carried out within the church. A detailed description of these Scripture-twisting interpretations is presented in my book *The Church's Desperate Need for Revival.*

HOMOSEXUAL POLITICS IN THE CHURCH

Homosexuals operate support groups and lobby organizations in all mainline denominations, as well as in other religions. Their organizations function in church colleges and seminaries. Gays and lesbians are regularly appointed to church boards and commissions in mainline churches. The growing influence of the homosexual lobby is like a giant tidal wave sweeping down upon an unsuspecting church. In the next few years, religious institutions, including Christian schools, will likely face legal challenges, based on so-called "hate laws" and discrimination statutes, requiring them to hire or retain homosexual employees.

The Evangelical Lutheran Church in America appointed several homosexuals to help create a position statement on human sexuality. When the ELCA's first draft of *The Church and Human Sexuality* was published, it created such a fire storm of protest across the church that the original task force had to be augmented with a special advisory panel and a team to write the second draft of the proposed statement.

The rejected statement endorsed masturbation as healthy, called the use of condoms by teens a "moral imperative," and encouraged the blessing of homosexual unions. The statement called on the church to abandon the concept of "loving the sinner, and hating the sin" in reference to homosexuality. It further suggested that a binding commitment, not a marriage license or ceremony, is the primary requirement for marriage. Similar efforts to sanction the homosexual lifestyle are taking place in most mainline bodies as homosexuals and their supporters labor to break down the will and resistance of church members.

HOMOSEXUAL ACTIVISTS AND THEIR STRATEGY

Homosexual activists in various denominations are often more astute than those who oppose them. If referendums to endorse portions of the homosexual agenda are defeated in church conventions, evangelicals go home and celebrate their victories; the homosexual lobby goes home to prepare for the next battle. When homosexual activists evaluate a lost referendum or resolution, they calculate the results to determine if there were fewer votes against them than the last time the issue was debated. As the losing margins grow smaller, they reason that victory will come if they continue the fight. This is why no matter how many times the homosexual agenda is considered and defeated at denominational conventions, the homosexual activists will be back to try again. They have successfully utilized the same strategy to influence the passage of local, state and national legislation.

Homosexual organizations, such as ACT-UP, think nothing of disrupting worship services and intimidating church members. In New York's St. Patrick's Cathedral, radical homosexual activists threw condoms at worshipers and desecrated the communion elements. Radical homosexuals hurled condoms at worshipers in a Colorado church in 1993. "The condoms were attached to packets of Kool-Aid upon which had been written, 'Remember Jonestown'."[19]

In March 1994, the Armitage Baptist Church in Chicago, known for its pro-life stand in that city, was the victim of a pro-abortion demonstration staged by several radical organizations, including homosexuals. According to the *US News and World Report*:

The sponsors included Queer Nation, an anarchist youth group, Sister Serpents (an underground women's collective) and the National Committee to Free Puerto Rican POWs and Political Prisoners. A few demonstrators wore patches that said "Feminist Witch" and "Support Vaginal Pride." One placard, the only nod toward humor, showed the face of Michael Griffin, killer of Dr. Gunn, with the slogan, "Life — what a beautiful sentence.".... The night before the rally, the slogan "Choice or Else" was sprayed on the church, and the church reported that rocks were thrown at the glass doors. ... The Armitage congregation is roughly 30 percent black, 30 percent Hispanic and 40 percent white.[20]

WHAT EVANGELICALS ARE SAYING

Within the next decade, most mainline churches will succumb to the homosexual campaign to have their deviant lifestyle endorsed, blessed and ordained. Some evangelical churches and leaders have already joined the ranks of those who embrace homosexuality as a "gift of God to be celebrated." In a letter to the editor, published in *Christianity Today*, Peggy Campolo, wife of Tony Campolo who teaches sociology at Eastern College, St. Davids, Pennsylvania, stated:

Many of us who believe the Bible to be the inspired word of God also believe that both the sexual identities and the committed relationships of our homosexual sisters and brothers are cause for celebration, rather than either regret or condemnation.

I am grateful to Stanton Jones for stating the basis of what we believe so clearly. He points out that what the Bible condemns is the "isolated act" of people of the same gender having sex with each other. Homosexuality, as a fundamental element of personal identity, is not what the Bible condemns.[21]

BREAKING THE BONDAGE OF SEXUAL DEVIANCY

There is help and hope for those who are under the bondage of deviant sexual behavior. Homosexuals are people for whom Christ died. It is our duty as Christians to lovingly witness God's law and gospel to them. Paul wrote:

Know ye not that the unrighteous shall not inherit the kingdom of God? Be not deceived: neither fornicators, nor idolaters, nor adulterers, nor effeminate, nor abusers of themselves with mankind, nor thieves, nor covetous, nor drunkards, nor revilers, nor extortioners, shall inherit the kingdom of God. And such were some of you: but ye are washed, but ye are sanctified, but ye are justified in the name of the Lord Jesus, and by the Spirit of our God (1 Corinthians 6:9-11).

The Bible teaches that all persons in bondage to any form of sin can be set free through the life-changing power of Jesus Christ. The word "effeminate" in the above passage is rightly translated "homosexual." Paul observed that they too had been washed, sanctified and justified through repentance and faith in Christ. As with any type of bondage, the chains are wrapped tightly. Those who are under the power of drugs, alcohol, or sex addictions may feel there is no way out. Yet today there are multitudes who can testify that they have been set free to live victorious lives through the transforming power of Jesus Christ.

A few years ago, I counseled a man with homosexual tendencies who had a wife and several children. He had first gone to a psychologist who advised him to leave his wife and give full expression to his homosexual desires. He came to my office a broken man. He loved his wife and children and wanted release from his bondage, not surrender to it. After several counseling sessions which included the Word of God and prayer, he yielded his heart to Jesus Christ in tearful repentance. Today he and his family are together, and he walks free of his former bondage.

Over the years, many homosexuals have sought help and counseling through Bible-believing churches, because they desire to be set free, not told that they have to live in or "celebrate" their bondage. Bible-based counseling centers and support groups across the nation are highly successful in helping gays and lesbians find new life in Christ.

If pastors would only step into their pulpits and declare the whole counsel of God — preaching the law to convict of sin and the gospel that sets the captive free — many could be unshackled from the bondage of sin and evil! That is the gospel described by Paul:

For I am not ashamed of the gospel of Christ: for it is the power of God unto salvation to every one that believeth; to the Jew first, and also to the Greek. For therein is the righteousness of God revealed from faith to faith: as it is written, The just shall live by faith (Romans 1:16,17).

THE ROLE OF HOMOSEXUALS IN THE CHURCH

Homosexuals should be warmly welcomed in Christian churches and treated with all courtesy. They should be invited to attend worship services where they may hear the Word of God, be converted and saved. Christians should reach out in friendship and kindness to gays and lesbians, witnessing the whole Word of God. Rejecting the lifestyle does not mean rejecting the sinner. Derogatory remarks about homosexuals should not flow from the lips of those who bear the name of Jesus Christ.

Homosexuals who have not repented and turned from their deviant lifestyle should not be permitted to receive Holy Communion, preach, teach, lead youth programs or hold office in the church. I do not suggest that homosexuals should be singled out for such discipline — the same policy should be applied to any person who is living in a willful state of sin. It brings shame on the church when Christian leaders or church members carry on immoral activities and are permitted to remain in positions of responsibility. The church must demand the highest ethical standards from all members, but especially those who bear positions of responsibility (1 Timothy 3).

THE BATTLE FOR LIFE

Christians who believe that abortion is just another issue among many other issues are gravely mistaken. The outcome of this conflict will inevitably determine the future of America. The Roe v. Wade decision of 1973 set the nation on a collision course with God's judgment. According to reports issued by the Right to Life Committee, 4,400 babies are killed by abortion every day; 1.6 million are killed every year; 31 million have been killed since abortion was legalized in 1973. Approximately 30 percent of all babies conceived in the United States are killed by abortion.

Personally, I am not sure that Sanctity of Life Sunday is such a good idea, though its purpose to stir the church to action is honorable. In many churches, sermons are preached about the value of human life, and literature is distributed — and that is good. Yet it seems this once-a-year event gives churches and Christians an opportunity to pay lip-service to this vital issue, then set it aside until the next Sanctity of Life Sunday rolls around. The church should be engaged in the battle for human life every day of the year.

Many Christians seem to be buying the feminist movement's lie that abortion is a matter of choice, a private decision between a woman and her doctor. In this land of ease and convenience, even our children are "disposable." Abortion is becoming the nation's answer to unwanted pregnancies and imperfect children. The pro-abortionists often link choice and quality of life when speaking about abortion rights, but aborted babies have no choice and no life at all, with or without quality. As a pro-life newsletter observed, "Every third baby dies from choice."

Compromising church statements on abortion declare, "Some believe this about abortion; others have a contrary opinion," as though Christians may rightly be on either side of this debate. The only side of this or any other issue that Christians should embrace is God's side. The Bible says nothing about our "right" to discard an unwanted child, but it clearly teaches that from conception to the grave, human life is sacred.

"Thou shalt not kill," is still a valid part of divine law, and no nation or individual may violate God's law without the certainty of incurring His wrath. Our Creator declares that He has knit us in our mother's womb, body and soul (Psalm 139:13,14). While we were still in the womb He knew us (Jeremiah 1:5). Jesus taught that life is precious. He came that we might have life abundantly (John 10:10). The Lord condemned those in Israel who offered their children to Molech:

> Whosoever he be of the children of Israel, or of the strangers that sojourn in Israel, that giveth any of his seed unto Molech; he shall surely be put to death: ... I will set my face against that man, and will cut him off from among his people; because he hath given of his seed unto Molech, to defile my sanctuary, and to profane my holy name (Leviticus 20:2,3).

The Bible describes the slaughter of Israel's children as an abomination:

> And they built the high places of Baal, which are in the valley

of the son of Hinnom, to cause their sons and their daughters to pass through the fire unto Molech; which I commanded them not, neither came it into my mind, that they should do this abomination, to cause Judah to sin (Jeremiah 32:35).

The Bible offers sufficient instruction for Christians to stand against abortion:

If thou forbear to deliver them that are drawn unto death, and those that are ready to be slain; If thou sayest, Behold, we knew it not; doth not he that pondereth the heart consider it? and he that keepeth thy soul, doth not he know it? and shall not he render to every man according to his works? (Proverbs 24:11,12).

FIVE FRONTS IN THE BATTLE TO END ABORTION

FRONT #1: National legislation. The law of the land legalizing abortion did not come from the halls of the Congress, but from the United States Supreme Court. The Roe v. Wade decision was based, not upon law, but on the misguided philosophies of members of the Court. Legislation must be passed granting protection to the unborn, even if it requires a Right to Life Amendment to the Constitution. It is amazing that the words of the Declaration of Independence can be so clear and yet so totally ignored in America's definition of human life:

We hold these Truths to be self-evident, that all Men are created equal, that they are endowed by their Creator with certain unalienable Rights, that among these are Life, Liberty, and the Pursuit of Happiness.

Under the Clinton administration's proposed health care plan, abortion will be offered as a standard benefit. Even if abortion benefits are dropped from consideration in the initial bill, liberal politicians and pro-abortion activists will surely press for its inclusion later. Individual Christians will pay for abortions through their taxes; churches and religious organizations will be required to fund abortions for their employees. Even now, abortions for federal government employees are being funded with tax dollars through the Federal Employee Health Benefits Program, passed by the Congress and signed by President Clinton.

Legislation against abortion is becoming increasingly unpopular, as abortion-rights activists try to convince the general public that "choice" is the only just solution. But what is most alarming are the laws and regulations being proposed and enacted to prevent non-profit organizations from speaking out on abortion or other social issues. Non-profit organizations are being threatened with the loss of their bulk-mailing permits and the loss of their tax-exempt status if they try to influence legislation. If these statutes are enacted and enforced, they will harm the effectiveness of most Christian ministries. Where are the ACLU and liberal denominations as these rights of free speech are being denied to conservative Christians? As Christians who still have the right to a secret ballot, we need to know where the politicians stand on the issue of abortion and vote only for those who uphold life.

FRONT #2: Abortion Clinics. There is nothing "clinical" about abortion clinics — they are more rightly called baby crematoriums. Clinics are about life and health, these centers are about death.

Protesters in front of abortion clinics are being driven away and intimidated by new laws and rulings aimed at eliminating opposition to abortion. The Supreme Court's ruling in 1994 that allows the Racketeer Influenced and Corrupt Organization Act (RICO) to be used to sue protesters who block women's access to abortion clinics was but another installment in the loss of freedoms for conservative Christians. It was followed by the Clinic Access Bill, passed by Congress and signed by President Clinton in May 1994. One by one, basic rights of free speech and peaceful protest are being taken away from those who oppose abortion. This too is part of the New World Order.

Some Christians have been sentenced to longer prison terms for protesting in front of an abortion clinic than convicted drug dealers. The media frequently refers to peaceful pro-life demonstrators in front of abortion clinics as "violent," while pro-abortion demonstrators are lauded as the "defenders of women's rights." If protests in front of abortion clinics do not continue, the pro-life movement will suffer a tremendous set-back.

It is my firm conviction that Christians should keep their protests within the law. America is a nation of laws, and we must never give way to anarchy. Violence committed against abortion-clinic doctors and staff members has not helped the pro-life movement, nor has the burning and vandalizing of abortion centers. All such violence should be both rejected and condemned by the Christian community.

Christians are instructed to obey those set over us (Romans 13:1-7). At the same time, "we ought to obey God rather than man" (Acts 5:29). No government is ever justified when asking its citizens to sin or to condone sinful acts. That principle was recognized by the international community at the Nuremberg trials following World War II when numerous Nazi leaders were held accountable for their actions, regardless of their government's orders. A few decades ago, American law defended segregation. Those who broke the laws of segregation in order to change those laws were prepared to pay the price. Christians whose consciences allow them to protest in ways that violate what they view to be unjust laws must likewise be prepared to bear the consequences of their actions. Even so, Christian are never justified in breaking one of God's laws to defend another.

FRONT #3: The churches. Most mainline churches are committed to a position of pro-abortion and choice. Every Christian in those churches should be working to change the position of their denominations to pro-life. If the denomination's position is not likely to be changed, members should withdraw and unite with a church body that stands on the principles of God's Word regarding this vital issue. It defies all logic that those who oppose abortion should be part of a church, political party or organization that endorses the wanton killing of the unborn.

FRONT #4: Care for unwed mothers and adoption. Christians should develop and support crisis pregnancy centers where unwed mothers who choose life will receive support to carry their babies to birth. Women need to know there are choices beyond abortion. Congregations should welcome, accept and shelter unwed mothers rather than judge them. Parents whose unwed daughters become pregnant should create a loving, accepting atmosphere in which their daughters can carry the babies to full term. Such acceptance does not mean approval of sin, but love for both the expectant mother and her child. Young families should consider the adoption of children born out of wedlock. There are countless children eagerly waiting for a family to adopt them.

Churches should also be supportive and helpful to women who have had abortions. Many suffer from psychological damage and guilt.

Through the Word of God, they need to be brought to repentance, forgiveness and wholeness. God's grace is sufficient.

FRONT #5: The Family. Family life was established by God. Strong and loving families are the greatest asset of any nation. Every home should be a safe haven for all who live there. Parents have an obligation to train their children in the nurture and admonition of the Lord. Christian parents need to instruct their children in the principles of God's Word regarding the sanctity of human life. Every home should have a family altar where God's Word is read and prayer for one another is offered.

Society should financially assist parents and families who are deserving, but laws and regulations promoting or encouraging broken families should be abolished. Under existing welfare laws, fathers are sometimes forced to withdraw from a home in order for their families to receive welfare benefits, and payments to unwed mothers are routinely increased with every child they bear. Every year thousands of fathers who abandon their wives and children are not required to financially provide for their needs. Legislation is needed to change these injustices and strengthen family life in America.

Whether the battle over abortion is long or short, whether we win or lose, Christians need to be faithful to the Word of God by standing fast for the sanctity of human life. All people will be required to give an account to Almighty God on certain matters — our stand for life will surely be one of them.

EUTHANASIA

Euthanasia is defined by Webster's New Universal Unabridged Dictionary as "the act of putting to death painlessly a person suffering from an incurable and painful disease or condition." Proponents of euthanasia like to define it as "death with dignity." Dr. Jack Kevorkian is not alone in his efforts to help those who want to terminate their lives. The Hemlock Society's popular suicide manual, *Final Exit*, details various ways people may end their lives. Support for the medical profession to carry out euthanasia on request is growing. Of course we must ask — at the request of whom?

While the above definition of active euthanasia involves "putting to death," passive euthanasia is defined as deliberately withholding life-sustaining measures, such as a feeding tube, in order to cause someone's death. Passive euthanasia is commonly practiced today.

Joseph Fletcher, whose book on situation ethics gave license to many liberal theologians to base their ethical positions on expediency rather than on the Word of God, is a strong advocate of euthanasia. In 1973, Fletcher made the following comments in the *American Journal of Nursing:*

> It is ridiculous to give ethical approval to the positive ending of sub-human life in utero as we do in the therapeutic abortions for reasons of mercy and compassion but refuse to approve of positively ending a sub-human life in extremis. If we are morally obliged to put an end to a pregnancy when an amniocentesis reveals a terribly defective fetus, we are equally obliged to put an end to a patient's hopeless misery when a brain scan reveals that a patient with cancer has advanced brain metastases.[22]

Francis Schaeffer asks:

> Will a society which has assumed the right to kill infants in the womb — because they are unwanted, imperfect, or merely inconvenient — have difficulty in assuming the right to kill other human beings, especially older adults who are judged unwanted, deemed imperfect physically or mentally, or considered a possible social nuisance?[23]

Unless conditions in America change for the better and soon, persons in their 50s and older are in great danger of having their lives terminated by a society whose value of human life is diminishing every day. How far are we from the time when keeping the aged alive will be based on their value to society or their cost of care? President Clinton, in a television interview, responded to a question from Tom Brokaw about the relationship of living wills and medical costs. According to the *U.S. News and World Report,* Clinton's answer was "jarring."

> There are "a lot of extra costs" in medical care at the end of life, and getting more Americans to sign living wills is "one way to weed some of them out," Clinton said last November.[24]

Dr. R. A. Gallop, head of the Food Science Department at the

University of Manitoba, was right when he warned that the acceptance of abortion would lead to the acceptance of euthanasia. He stated:

> Once you permit the killing of the unborn child, there will be no stopping. There will be no age limit. You are setting off a chain reaction that will eventually make you the victim. Your children will kill you because you permitted the killing of their brothers and sisters. Your children will kill you because they will not want to support you in your old age. Your children will kill you for your homes and estates. If a doctor will take money for killing the innocent in the womb, he will kill you with a needle when paid by your children. This is the terrible nightmare you are creating for the future.[25]

Without question, once euthanasia is accepted, it will be broadened to include more and more people who are required to die for the benefit of society. In the Netherlands where euthanasia is legal, doctors now routinely "kill without the patient's knowledge or consent ... In 45 percent of cases of involuntary euthanasia in hospitals, doctors didn't even consult family members."[26] The Dutch Pediatric Association "has issued instructions allowing euthanasia for babies who are not terminally ill but simply face chronic sickness or mental retardation."[27]

WHEN THEY WON'T LET YOU DIE

The other side of euthanasia is not being allowed to die. Most of us hope that we will be able to avoid a lingering, painful death when our time comes, but such matters are not in our power to control. As difficult as the sudden death of a loved one may be, there is always a measure of comfort in knowing they did not have to suffer.

Modern medical technology is neither moral nor immoral; what we do with the technology is the issue. "Pulling the plug" to deliberately take a person's life is one thing, forcing someone to remain beyond the appointed time of death is another. Today hospitals and doctors are so fearful of law suits that helpless patients are forced to linger —sometimes in pain and suffering — with wires, tubes and artificial life-support machines that extend life far beyond the point when death would naturally occur. The decisions over what measures to take or not to take can be very difficult for families and the medical profession when dealing with terminal patients, but the underlying duty of man is to sustain life while life is sustainable and to accept death when it is not. I am not suggesting that it is ever acceptable to engage in any type of passive euthanasia where vital treatments are withheld so that family members or the medical profession control when a person is to die. I simply state that death is natural, and there is an appointed time for each of us to die.

In this age of technological wonders and medical marvels, more people are likely to die in hospitals than ever before. Yet something precious is lost in not being able to die in one's own home with loved ones gathered around. I am personally thankful for the hospice concept which recognizes the intrinsic value of such a passing, but the hospice setting could become a terrible place if euthanasia is ever legalized in this country.

TRUE COMPASSION IN DEATH

"Precious in the sight of the Lord is the death of his saints" (Psalm 116:15). As one who has pastored for over 30 years and witnessed the deaths of many people, I understand the pain and helpless feeling of those who must stand by and watch a loved one suffer through a terminal illness. In those cases, death often comes not only with deep sorrow but with an overwhelming sense of release. Yet the Bible is clear, there is "a time to be born and a time to die ..." (Ecclesiates 3:2). The Word of God further teaches, "Seeing his days are determined, the number of his months are with thee, thou hast appointed his bounds that he cannot pass" (Job 14:5). And a clear word is given in Psalm 68:20, "... unto God the Lord belong the issues from death."

True believers in Christ approach death with confidence, "... though I walk through the valley of the shadow of death, I will fear no evil: for thou art with me ..." Psalm 23: 4). For the Christian, death is but a door leading to eternal life with the Lord. When we get to heaven, we shall not waste our eternity exchanging horror stories of how bad things were for us on earth. We shall not retrace the steps of the sorrows and anguish we suffered on earth, but we shall "blend our voices with the angels and the archangels and all the company of heaven," and we shall be "lost in wonder, love and praise" for ever and ever.

And God shall wipe away all tears from their eyes; and there shall be no more death, neither sorrow, nor crying, neither shall there be any more pain: for the former things are passed away (Revelation 21:4).

The battle over euthanasia is before us. The opening salvos have already been fired. As our society continues to divest itself of any connection with biblical values, ethical decisions will be formulated by humanistic considerations. Only Christians anchored in the Word of God will be able to offer credible alternatives to the nation's dilemmas. If the trend to jettison God from national life proceeds in the future as it has in the past, it is not likely that our Christian views will be given much consideration. But may there never be a time in America when the witness of God's Word regarding life and hope is not heard!

FROM GREENLAND'S ICY MOUNTAINS

From Greenland's icy mountains,
   from India's coral strand,
Where Afric's sunny fountains
   roll down their golden sand,
From many an ancient river,
   from many a palmy plain,
They call us to deliver their land
   from error's chain.

Can we whose souls are lighted
   with wisdom from on high,
Can we to men benighted
   the lamp of life deny?
Salvation, O salvation!
   The joyful sound proclaim,
Till each remotest nation
   has learned Messiah's Name.

Waft, waft, ye winds, his story,
   and you, ye waters roll,
Till, like a sea of glory,
   it spreads from pole to pole;
Till o'er our ransomed nature
   the Lamb for sinners slain,
Redeemer, King, Creator,
   in bliss returns to reign.

Reginald Heber, 1783-1826

Chapter 8

Contending for the Faith — Against the One-World Religion

And I beheld another beast coming up out of the earth; and he had two horns like a lamb and he spake as a dragon. And he exerciseth all the power of the first beast before him, and causeth the earth and them which dwell therein to worship the first beast, whose deadly wound was healed (Revelation 13:11,12).

Efforts to establish a one-world religion are moving at an alarming pace. Few Christians are aware of the diabolical steps already taken by world-religion leaders to usher in the utopian age of unified spirituality. Liberal mainline churches, Protestant and Catholic, are now leagued with pagan religions to create the framework for the new global faith. The New Age movement is dedicated to this purpose. This global vision does not require the actual unification of world religions or even their blending, but a shared sense of purpose, toleration and mutual cooperation. No religion will be permitted to consider its creeds or teachings to be superior to any other in the global community. Joint-worship services and cooperative interfaith programs are becoming commonplace, even at the local level.

THE INTERFAITH THREAT

Cooperation with world religions has become fashionable among those who believe that no religion has more spiritual claims than another. Interfaith organizations abound throughout the world. Cooperation and dialogue with non-Christian religions is high on the agenda of the World Council of Churches. Pope John Paul II, a strong believer in interfaith cooperation, has sponsored and participated in prayer services that have included Buddhists and Moslems. Vatican II declared that while Catholicism is true, other religions are legitimate. Robert Runcie, former Archbishop of Canterbury, stated:

> Religion taken as a whole benefited much from the variety in its different forms. All the centuries that the Spirit of God had been working in Christians, He must also have been working in Hindus, Buddhists, Muslims, and others ... it takes humility and sincerity to concede that there is a certain incompleteness in each of our traditions ... This will mean that some claims about the exclusiveness of the church will have to be renounced.[1]

Efforts to establish a one-world religion represent the greatest single threat to the church in our times. Dissent is minimal, with few voices being raised to sound the alarm. I believe that the coming one-world religion prophesied in the Book of Revelation is not some event yet to take place far out in the future. It is being constructed now with unbelievable speed.

ONE-WORLD RELIGION —
THE CULMINATION OF FALSE TEACHINGS
AND PRACTICES

Liberal church leaders have watered down and, in some cases, abandoned biblical Christianity in order to embrace global ecumenical unity. The cooperation of Christianity with world religions is the ultimate culmination of false teachings and the denial of biblical doctrines. Every doctrinal departure since the days of the Apostles has been directed toward this goal by the enemy of men's souls, regardless of the knowledge or intent of those who espoused them.

Biblical inerrancy was among the first foundational doctrines to be jettisoned. Once the Bible was no longer taken seriously in liberal churches, other doctrines were easily set aside. Efforts to bring Christianity into conformity with world religions demand that numerous biblical teachings be changed or abandoned. Doctrines concerning Christ — His virgin birth, deity, blood-atonement for the sins of the world, His resurrection, ascension, and the promise of His return to earth to judge the world — have all been set aside so that Jesus Christ will become acceptable to other religions as just another great religious leader among other great religious leaders. The doctrine of universalism which affirms the salvation of all people regardless of their faith in Jesus

Christ is also necessary if unity with other religions is to be achieved.

THE STAGE IS SET FOR THE ANTICHRIST

The global economy, the one-world government and the one-world religion form the antichrist's unholy trinity. They are bonded together essentially by the same people. Read the rosters of the Trilateral Commission, the Club of Rome, the Parliament of World Religions, the Temple of Understanding, Thanksgiving Square, the World Conference on Religion and Peace and a host of New Age groups, and you will discover many leaders interconnected with several organizations.

The partnership of government and religion is described in the Book of Revelation when a world dictator will join with the world-religion leader to rule the nations. The apostate church described in Revelation 17 as the great whore engages in the magic arts, sexual immorality and the worship of idols. While that description may have been difficult to comprehend only a few years ago, it is an accurate portrayal of portions of organized Christianity today.

The global economy now in place already binds the destinies of men and nations. When the global economic depression comes (and it will come) and when world peace is shattered (and it will be shattered), the cries for a world dictator will sound from the four corners of the earth. The beast out of the sea and the beast out of the land will come to power with lightning speed. "And all that dwell upon the earth shall worship him, whose names are not written in the book of life of the Lamb slain from the foundation of the world" (Revelation 13:8).

CONSERVATIVE CHRISTIANS ARE BEING SET UP FOR PERSECUTION

Members of conservative churches who conclude that the new global religion poses no threat to them are in for a rude awakening. Bible-believing Christians are the enemy of the New World Order. Those who believe in moral absolutes are already viewed as "radical fundamentalists" and a danger to society. Only Bible-believing Christians stand in the way of globalist efforts to secularize America. In a time not so distant, persons who confess Jesus Christ as the world's only Savior will face bitter persecution.

Even now, Bible-believing Christians with exclusive views of Christianity are being identified with the radical fundamentalists of other religions, including terrorists. According to this linkage, Christian protesters in front of abortion clinics and the radical Moslems who bombed the World Trade Center are all cast from the same mold. The identification of conservative Christians as dangerous religious zealots is intended to isolate and later to eradicate Christian influence from the world scene. A study on "fundamentalism" sponsored by the American Academy of Arts and Sciences was evaluated by George W. Cornell:

Scholars say the world, previously presumed advancing into an enlightened age of sheer rationalism free of religious throwbacks, has instead encountered a global storm of religious fundamentalism ... It has shocked modern secular states, overturned prior analyses and sent splintering tremors through societies around the earth, according to an international team of experts ... They say the unforeseen, religion-linked turmoil seems everywhere — in biblical "inerrancy" and Operation Rescue crusades in this country, Christian violence in Ireland, West Bank Jewish expansionism, Buddhist militancy in Sri Lanka, Christian-Muslim battling in ex-Communist states, Muslim absolutism in Iran and Sudan, and Hindu rampages in India ... "We have hurricane-force winds of the spirit, blowing in unpredictable places," says the Rev. Martin E. Marty (ELCA), noted church historian and editor of a massive, multivolume examination of the rash of modern fundamentalisms.[2]

A Supreme Court decision in January 1994 affirmed the right of the pro-abortionists to sue protesters who block women's access to abortion clinics, using a federal racketeering law. The same law written to control organized crime is now being used against Christian groups such as Operation Rescue. The Racketeer Influenced and Corrupt Organization Act (RICO) can now be used against anybody who uses free speech in ways that are offensive to ultra-liberal groups or individuals. So-called "hate laws" which are being passed throughout the country to "protect" homosexuals may be applied to silence those who speak or write against homosexuality as an acceptable lifestyle.

Seven seminars sponsored by People for the American Way and the Association of School Administrators took place in 1993 throughout the United States, using the theme "Responding Democratically To Opposition Groups." The opposition groups they had in mind were, of course, mostly conservative Christians. People for the American Way provided videos to "expose" the Christian Coalition, the Free Congress Foundation, Focus on the Family, Citizens for Excellence in Education and Concerned Women for America. One seminar speaker at the session in Greensboro, North Carolina, stated that because of censorship and attacks on the Rainbow Curriculum's *Heather Has Two Mommies,* it was prevented from being used in the New York City schools.[3] Christians should be encouraged by such reports, knowing that the opposition becomes frightened when God's people stand for biblical principles.

THE NEW AGE MOVEMENT

The New Age movement is massive. If you have any doubt, walk into any secular bookstore and look at the shelf space devoted to New Age publications. The New Age movement is a religion as well as a global political lobby. It does not have a headquarters, nor is it identified by any single leader. It exists through hundreds of organizations and thousands of like-minded individuals who labor for global unity in religion and government. Many New Age organizations represent the vital link between those who desire a one-world government and those who desire a one-world religion.

It is not possible in the limited context of this book to present a detailed description of the New Age movement, although in various chapters we have included important information regarding its agenda and tactics. Many excellent books exposing the New Age movement are listed in the bibliography. My concern here is to show how the New Age movement is making inroads into the churches in order to achieve its goal of a one-world religion. The New Age movement is a most effective tool of Satan to spiritually enslave masses of humanity. Christians need to become informed about the New Age agenda, and stand against its Satan-inspired attempts to deceive the church.

NEW AGE PERSONALITIES AND ORGANIZATIONS

A networking of New Age organizations now crosses the boundaries of religion and politics. Some well-known names frequently associated with the New Age include: the Dalai Lama, Matthew Fox, Marilyn Ferguson, Rosemary Reuther, Robert Muller, David Spangler, Gerald O. Barney, Diana Eck, Donald Keys, Thomas Merton, Betty Friedan, Mary Daly, Ted Turner, John Denver, Barbara Marx Hubbard, Lester Brown, Jose Arguelles (associated with Earth Day) and Alice Bailey. Major New Age organizations with a global agenda include: Planetary Citizens, the Temple of Understanding, World-Watch Institute, Better World Society, World Goodwill and Lucis Trust.

NEW AGE NEW-SPEAK

New Age vocabulary is common in church pulpits and political speeches as well as in radio and television programming, though many do not recognize its origin. Eastern mysticism and religious teachings are blended with Christian thought by those involved in the promotion of this global religion. New Age concepts include: The New World Order, the global society, Mother Earth (Gaia), holistic (referring to medicine and spirituality), imaging, visualization, channeling, the god within, goddesses, spiritual healing, spiritual journeys, just to name a few. A New Age retreat on the theme "A Personal Liberation Spirituality" was promoted as follows:

> This retreat provides a safe place for people to explore, re-define, re-affirm, re-structure and re-state their spirituality. It is a chance to own or disown and to move on. It is a chance to put some closure on parts of your spiritual life and to celebrate other parts.[4]

Ted Peters, a theology professor at Pacific Lutheran Theological Seminary (ELCA) , has written books and articles on the New Age movement. Peters has few unkind things to say about New Age, but he strongly chides conservative Christians who fear it. According to Peters, evangelicals who write or preach that all New Age is the work of Satan may be lessening the seriousness of Satanism. "I may say these things are stupid, but you're not going to lose your soul over them," said Peters.[5] However, D. L. Cuddy, Ph.D., a commentator whose writings are syndicated in newspapers across the nation and who is surely one of the most informed critics of the New Age movement, states:

The purpose of this New Age movement is ultimately to have a one-world government, and it may be facilitated through what Lucis Trust calls the "science of service." World Goodwill (and the New Group of World Servers) is an arm of Lucis Trust and had as one of its "transition activities" the "Planetary Citizens Registry" or Planetary Citizens, which sponsored "Planetary Initiative for the World We Choose." An honorary chairman of Planetary Citizens was Norman Cousins, who is now president of World Federalist Association and said, "World Government is coming. In fact, it is inevitable. No arguments for or against it can change that fact."[6]

The Evangelical Lutheran Church in America has frequently employed New Age concepts in its teaching and worship. A bulletin insert mailed to congregations from ELCA headquarters in Chicago encouraged pastors to use the pagan "Prayer of Four-Directions" during a worship service. (The ELCA's "Guidelines for Inclusive Use of the English Language" directs pastors and writers not to use the word "pagan.") During the prayer, worshipers are asked to turn to each of the four directions and pray to the "Great Spirit."

At a worship service during an ELCA convention, participants were introduced to "smudging," a native-American practice involving the burning of sweet grass, sage and cedar. In the smoke-filled auditorium, worshipers were given an opportunity to offer the "Prayer to the Four-Directions." In addition, they sang "Bring Many Names" which refers to God as "Strong Mother God," "Old aching God," and "Young growing God."[7]

A worship service at a Pacifica Synod Convention (ELCA) opened with the blowing of a conch shell, followed by the singing of a pagan hymn or fertility chant.

It is night gliding through the passage
 Of an opening, a stream of water is the food of plants
It is the god who enters; not as a human does God enter:
 Male for the narrow waters
Female for the broad waters.[8]

KYTHING

Many feminists are devotees of New Age teachings. Consequently, New Age programs such as kything, yoga and transcendental meditation are frequently found in mainline churches today. Increasingly, liberal pastors include New Age teachings in their preaching and educational courses. It is not unusual to see church ads in local papers inviting people to participate in New Age programs. An ad for a retreat center in Minnesota, which involves people associated with the Evangelical Lutheran Church in America, stated that they were "linking ancient truths with contemporary wisdom seeking to weave a spirituality for today and into the 21st century." Encircling the ad in small print were the names of religious leaders whose "insights" would be explored at the conference. The names included: Matthew Fox, the Dalai Lama, Jesus, Hazel Henderson and Black Elk.[9]

A New Age program promoted by some mainline churches is kything. Kything (rhymes with tithing) is a technique whereby people are able to connect with one another "spirit to spirit or heart to heart". Supposedly kything may take place between persons living or dead, between persons and animals, and between persons and plants. Hillary Clinton is apparently into kything and channeling through conversations with Eleanor Roosevelt. Hillary stated that she gets advice from Eleanor. It was described by Jeanne Williams in *USA Today* as follows:

> And the first lady said that imaginary conversations with her role model, Eleanor Roosevelt, helped her get through the traumatic campaign year. Hillary said her mental chats with Eleanor were "one of the saving graces I have hung on to for dear life. ..." She went from asking Eleanor, "Why me?" to "how did you put up with this?"
>
> Then Hillary said she had "a wonderful revelation: Eleanor shook her head and said in my mind, "You know, I thought that would have been solved by now — you are just going to have to get out there and do it and don't make any excuses about it."[10]

The practice of kything was presented at a women's retreat sponsored by a Midwest congregation of the Evangelical Lutheran Church in America. Program materials included *The Art of Spiritual Presence* by Louis M. Savory and Patricia H. Berne. The authors stated in the preface: "To us kything is a most powerful basic spiritual skill, offering a way for members of the conspiracy of love to be consciously joined to each other, spirit to spirit."[11]

In their book Savory and Berne told of a man kything with an oak tree.

One young man during recuperation of burnout used to kythe with a large oak tree in a nearby park. Each day he would sit near the tree and connect with it spirit to spirit. He became aware of how it lifted its branches toward heaven, opening its leaves to all the energy of the sun, the air, and the rain ... Plants, flowers and trees have certain energies and qualities that we can use for our healing and wholeness.[12]

According to Savory and Berne, Jesus was into kything.

It is our belief that Jesus was not only familiar with what we call kything, but that it was an important part of his vision of the kingdom of God. During Jesus' final discourse at the Passover Supper he makes striking use of the preposition "in." We feel that he used this preposition to describe spirit-to-spirit or soul-to-soul presence that was to characterize relationships in the kingdom of God. "Do you believe that I am *in* the Father and the Father is *in* me?" In Christ, it is just as easy to kythe with someone on the other side of life as with someone on the other side of town.[13]

D.L.Cuddy observes that the Lord truly has the last word regarding the New Age strategists.

Concerning the "New Age" elite social engineers who want to take us into the arms of a New World Order, we should remember Revelation 17:13 which says: "These have one mind, and shall give their power and strength unto the beast." However, we should also be joyful that the next verse in Revelations proclaims that "The Lamb shall overcome them: for he is Lord of lords, and King of kings."[14]

THE PARLIAMENT OF WORLD RELIGIONS

The first Parliament of World Religions was convened in 1893. Leaders of many religions came together in Chicago to promote cooperation and understanding between peoples of different faiths. Some have labeled the first Parliament as a "watershed event in American history," because it prompted the beginning of an interfaith dialogue and cooperation among the world's religions. With so many religious wars and conflicts, creating understanding and good will among the peoples of various religions might seem like laudable goals. But the mere promotion of good will and understanding were never the intention of those who organized the first Parliament of World Religions. Their plan from the beginning was to lay the groundwork for building a global faith. At the first Parliament, Swami Vivekananda set the stage for interfaith gatherings by proclaiming that all the world's religions worshiped the same god, calling him by many names.

The second Parliament of World Religions took place in late summer of 1993, also in Chicago. The same lofty goals of promoting "understanding and good will" were expressed as the motive for the second gathering, but the program could not disguise the real intent of the organizers to advance a global government and a global religion. Over 6000 people representing at least 125 religions from around the world participated in the week-long program. The content of the Parliament's sessions revealed their agenda for world government and global religious solidarity.

Participants in the Parliament of World Religions included Christians, Hindus, Buddhists, Jains, Confucianists, Taoists, Zoroastrians, Jews, Moslems, Mormons, Wiccans, (witches) Theosophists and numerous New Age organizations. Leaders from the Evangelical Lutheran Church in America, the United Methodist Church, the United Church of Christ, the Disciples of Christ, the Presbyterian Church U.S.A., the Roman Catholic Church and many other Christian bodies, including Pentecostals, participated with witches, voodoo priests, atheists, New Agers, the Fellowship of Isis, and leaders of pagan religions. The National Council of Churches was also a co-sponsor of the Parliament.

The Roman Catholic Church was represented by several leaders, including Cardinal Joseph Bernardin, archbishop of Chicago. Archbishop Francesco Gioia, a Vatican official, presented the official position of Rome on religious dialogue. Mother Teresa was unable to attend because of health problems. "You are doing God's work," she told the Council's executive director, Daniel Gomez Ibanez, in a phone conversation. "I wanted to come very much. I know that your work is very important because you are working for the glory of God and the good of the whole world."[15]

An address at the closing session by the Dalai Lama, Tibetan Buddhist leader, drew over 20,000 people. The Dalai Lama actively promotes "a spiritual New World Order and the unity of all faiths, religions and sects."

Robert Muller gave the first plenary address entitled "Interfaith Understanding." Muller, former assistant secretary-general of the United Nations, blended New Age politics and New Age religion for the assembled delegates. Muller has long associations with the New Age movement as well as world-government groups. In his book *The New Genesis,* Muller stated:

> I have come to believe firmly today that our future peace, justice, and fulfillment, happiness and harmony on this planet will not depend on world government but on divine or cosmic government.
> ... my great personal dream is to get a tremendous alliance between all major religions and the U.N.[16]

In an article published in the World Good Will Newsletter, Muller stated:

> Religions and spiritual traditions: the world needs you very much! You, more than anyone else, have experience, wisdom, insights and feeling for the miracle of life, of the Earth and of the universe. After having been pushed aside in many fields of human endeavour, you must again be the lighthouse, the guides, the prophets and messengers of the ultimate mysteries of the universe and eternity. You must set up the mechanisms to agree, and you must give humanity the divine or cosmic rules for our behaviour on this planet.[17]

Patrick Henry, director of the Evangelical Lutheran Church in America's Institute for Ecumenical and Cultural Research, was quoted as saying to the Parliament: "The fear some Christians have of syncretism (mixing different beliefs) needs to be balanced against a fear that we might miss some new wisdom that God has to impart."[18]

THE INSTITUTE FOR 21ST CENTURY STUDIES AND THE PARLIAMENT

A principal sponsor of the Parliament of World Religions was the Institute for 21st Century Studies, founded by Dr. Gerald O. Barney in 1983. The Institute "promotes inter-regional and global cooperation on achieving sustainable economic and ecologic development and national security." According to the Institute's own literature their funding comes from "several U.S. foundations, especially the Rockefeller Brothers Fund, the Hewlett Foundation, and the Trinity Grants Program, UNESCO, the World Bank, UN Development Program, International Development Research Centre, the Evangelical Lutheran Church in America, and from several individuals and corporations."

Gerald O. Barney, founder and executive director of the Institute for 21st Century Studies, once headed Global 2000 commissioned by President Jimmy Carter. He is also a member of the Club of Rome. The Club of Rome, founded in 1968, is politically leftist, New Age and globalistic. It began with 30 individuals from 10 nations, endeavoring to provide answers to global concerns. The Club of Rome endorsed global economic management, population control and the redistribution of wealth.

The Institute for 21st Century Studies is linked with other organizations known for their focus on the New Age, one-world political agenda. Lester Brown, a former board member of the Institute and now serving on their advisory board, is president of World-Watch Institute, an organization which promotes one-world government.

Gerald Barney, a member of the Evangelical Lutheran Church in America, spoke to the Parliament delegates on the theme, "Global 2000 Revisited: What Shall We do?" Barney commented:

Many people doubt that there is a sustainable, just and humane future for Earth and her people. ... Christianity is not a sustainable faith as practiced now (e.g., the Catholic church's opposition to birth control and the biblical teaching that man is to take dominion over the Earth). Every person must learn to think like Earth, to act like Earth, to be Earth. As a part of this learning process we must all think through how our part of Earth can contribute to the new ... What laws must be changed, what traditions, what beliefs, what institutions?[19]

PARLIAMENT SESSIONS

Several times during the week, the Parliament's assembly hall was filled with smoke from the incense of Eastern groups that gave participants a sample of their worship practices. The delegates were asked to chant and hum New Age and Eastern exercises. The Wiccans went to Grant Park where, under a full moon, they marked off a large sacred circle and engaged in their rituals. The fact that Christians, including evangelicals, took part in the Parliament of World Religions with witches and voodoo priests shows how far the church's slide toward idolatry has moved.

Titles of the Parliament sessions reveal the nature and intent of their one-world religion agenda.

Establishing a Righteous Order Agreeable to All Religions

Christianity 'Born Again' for a New Age

The Spiritual Dimension of a Sustainable World Order

Religion in the Year 2020: A Worldwide Confederation of Interfaith Villages

The Impact of the World's Religions on the Ethics of Business in a Global Economy

The Near-Death Experience as a Basis for Religious Unity

Discerning the Universal Foundation of Religions

The Universal Word and Unity of Religions: Interfaith Harmony in the Global Society

The Parliament of World Religions — a U.N. of Religions

The Unity of Religion

The Return of the Goddess: Ecology, Spirituality and Partnership

Gods, Goddesses, Goblins: An Introduction to the Celtic Fairy Faith

The Role of the Priestess/Priest in the Fellowship of Isis

Zoroastrianism — An Ancient Religion for Modern Man

The Divine Union of Spirit and Nature

Wiccan Wisdom and the Environmental Crisis

Humanism, an Alternative to Traditional Religion

The Witch as Shaman: Rediscovering the Ancient Shamanistic Traditions of Europe

The Christ of the Twenty-first Century

Praying with Feminine Images of God

Voodoo in Haiti

Wiccan Devotionals

Insights into the Wisdom of the Divine Mother

THE DECLARATION OF A GLOBAL ETHIC

The primary document to come out of the Parliament of World Religions was the "Declaration of a Global Ethic," an attempt to define a common set of values for all nations and faiths. The declaration was largely drafted by Hans Küng, an ultra-liberal Roman Catholic theologian. He told representatives of the press:

> It is certainly the first time in history of humankind that a body of this importance tries to lay down principles for understanding, principles for behavior which ... can also be supported by non-believers. There was no objection to any important point, and that was a happy surprise.[20]

The document declares: "We are the women and men who have embraced the precepts and practices of the world's religions. The core values of the religions form the basis of the global ethic." The statement maintains that there is a "consensus of values, irrevocable standards and fundamental moral attitudes." The document condemns "representatives of religions who dismiss other religions as of little value." Küng explained that the document does not mention God so as not to exclude any religion that does not recognize a supreme being.[21]

THE PARLIAMENT'S WORK CONTINUES

We have not heard the last of the Parliament of World Religions by any means. An ongoing Council, board and staff labor diligently to carry on the Parliament's agenda. They recently announced in their newsletter an idea for a Sunday school curriculum on interfaith under-standing.[22] Again, we see that children are the targets of the global movement. They must, of course, be carefully taught. Bible-believing parents who are members of liberal denominations had better pay closer attention to what goes on in their children's Sunday school classes.

PROJECT GLOBAL 2000

Global 2000, inspired by Robert Muller and Margaret Mead in 1978, has been launched by a networking of global and New Age organiza-tions. It was initially coordinated by Global Education Associates, but now its advocates include world religion leaders and the United Na-tions. Its work has been ongoing. In October 1991, a meeting of Global 2000 in Vienna produced six councils to enlist six major sectors of society in "common efforts for policies and systems commensurate to the global-scale realities confronting the human community." The six councils are: Education, Youth, Religion, Business, Health and Com-munications. Their goal is "to create world order systems that are equitable, inclusive, and ecologically sustainable."[23] It is imperative to understand the connection between the goals of Project 2000 and the goals of the Parliament of World Religions.

According to published reports, Project Global 2000 will be pro-moted in two stages. The first stage, set to operate from 1991 to 1993, endeavored to establish coordinated global policies. The second stage, from 1994 to 2000, will seek the implementation of those same policies, as well as other coordinated efforts to achieve global cooperation in education, environmental issues, religion, and world peace.

A major player in Project Global 2000 is the World Conference on Religion and Peace. Organized in 1968 the WCRP is one of the world's largest and most active interfaith organizations. Leaders from major Christian bodies are involved in the WCRP's one-world religion, one-world government agenda.

The World Conference on Religion and Peace joined other globalist organizations in a symposium entitled "The United Nations in an In-terdependent World," July 11-16, 1994. Other sponsors included: UNICEF, UNESCO, UN Center for Disarmament Affairs, UN Envi-ronment Programme, UN Population Fund, New York City Board of Education, Educators for Social Responsibility, Friends of the United

Nations, International Institutes for Peace Education, World Federalist Association and World Order Models Project.[24] It is alarming to see the magnitude of these globalist efforts. The United Nations officially works with numerous religious organizations to promote its one-world government agenda.

THE TEMPLE OF UNDERSTANDING

The Temple of Understanding, a global interfaith association headquartered at the Cathedral of St. John the Divine in New York City, was founded in 1960 by Juliet Hollister, with the support of Eleanor Roosevelt, Pope John XXIII, Secretary-General U Thant, Dr. Albert Schweitzer, Thomas Merton and the Dalai Lama. It has spun off other global organizations including the Global Forum of Spiritual and Parliamentary Leaders for Human Survival, the North American Interfaith Network and the Hartley Film Foundation. It cooperates with the United Nations to sponsor monthly round tables at the United Nations secretariat. It works with religious and non-governmental organizations "to further the work of the United Nations."[25]

Their association with the Hartley Film Foundation enables them to promote New Age, interfaith teachings in the public schools with help from many high officials. The Hartley films feature information produced and presented by some of the most ardent supporters of the New Age movement. The Temple of Understanding's programs are blatant in their one-world religion, one-world government agenda. Their benefactors, donors and supporters consist of thousands of the nation's richest and most influential citizens.

Interfaith services are common at the Cathedral of St. John the Divine. The Dalai Lama has appeared there often enough to be mistaken for a pastor of the church. Dr. Karan Singh, Chairman of the Temple of Understanding, said that "there is only one truth and the wise seek it through many paths." The Temple of Understanding was a co-sponsor of the Parliament of World Religions.

THANKSGIVING SQUARE

A structure in the center of Dallas, Texas, resembles the Tower of Babel. The tower is part of a park-like complex known as Thanksgiving

Square. Constructed in 1977, it offers people of various world religions a place to gather for prayer. The National Thanksgiving Commission, headquartered at Thanksgiving Square, has loose connections with the United Nations. Former President Gerald Ford called Thanksgiving Square "a major national shrine." Former President George Bush referred to it as "a symbol and a home for America's most beloved tradition."[26] In fact, it is a monument to the one-world religion.

An advertisement from the National Thanksgiving Commission displayed 100 world-religion leaders who endorsed the movement. The list includes: The Rev. Dr. Herbert W. Chilstrom, Bishop of the Evangelical Lutheran Church in America; Ameganvi Aveglui, High Priest of the Sacred Forest, Togo, Africa; Swami Bhavyananda, Ramakrishna Order of India, London; Edward Carpenter, Dean, Westminster Abbey, London; Dr. Diana Eck, Professor of Religions, Harvard University; Tamal Krishna Goswami, Governing Body Commissioner International Society for Krishna Consciousness; The Ven. Dr. Henepola Gunaratana, Director, Washington Buddhist Vihara; His Holiness, Tenzin Gyatso, the Fourteenth Dalai Lama; Dr. Viqar A. Hamdani, Representative to the United Nations, World Muslim Congress; Juliet Hollister, founder of the Temple of Understanding; His Holiness, Pope John Paul II; Rev. Patricia McClurg, President, National Council of Churches USA; Henri J.M. Nouwen, Priest at Daybreak, Toronto; Rev. Sri Swami Satchidananda, Distinguished Hindu Monk, Satchidananda Ashram; Thich-Tam-Chau, Supreme Patriarch World Vietnamese Buddhist Order, Montreal; Dr. Cynthia C. Wedel, President, World Council of Churches.

Thanksgiving Square certainly has more ambitious interests than merely promoting Thanksgiving Day in this or any other country. The word "Thanksgiving" is only a ruse to disguise their global agenda and the promotion of interfaith activity. A statement included with the pictures of the hundred world-religion leaders reads:

THESE 100 VOICES FROM EVERY CONTINENT
SPEAK FOR ALL OF US IN A YEARLY
DECLARATION OF THANKSGIVING.
AS A THANKFUL PERSON I AM ONLY ONE —
BUT I AM AT-ONE-MENT WITH BILLIONS OF PEOPLE
AROUND THE WORLD WHO ARE GRATEFUL

TO THE LORD OF CREATION —
ONE WITH THE BASIC GRATITUDE OF
ALL WORLD RELIGIONS,
ONE WITH MILLIONS OF THANKFUL FAMILIES,
THOUSANDS OF GRATEFUL COMMUNITIES,
HUNDREDS OF REVERENT CULTURES,
AND A FEW NATIONS
WITH OFFICIAL THANKSGIVINGS.
NOW WE SHARE AT-ONE-MENT WITH A WORLD
DECLARING THANKS TOGETHER, REPRESENTED BY NEW
PEOPLE EACH YEAR FROM AROUND THE GLOBE SAYING,
LORD I WILL PRAISE THEE AMONG THE NATIONS.

The use of the word "at-one-ment" in the preceding statement, a play on the word "atonement," is used in ecumenical circles to portray unity. This unholy alliance of false religions has usurped a precious word of the holy Christian faith which centers on our Lord's divine act of redemption, and they are using it to promote the one-world religion. The word "Lord" in the above statement must be a composite god of the globalists.

Each year the Thanksgiving Commission issues a Declaration of Thanksgiving and invites 12 world-religion leaders to sign it. The Declaration of Thanksgiving in 1989 stated in part:

WE, THE PEOPLE
OF MANY TRADITIONS OVER THE EARTH,
ARE DEEPLY CONSCIOUS THAT FOR MANY CENTURIES
THE SPIRIT OF THANKSGIVING TO THE SOURCE
OF INFINITE GOODNESS
HAS CREATED A CENTER FOR OUR LIVES ...
WE REJOICE THAT GRATITUDE IS A REALITY
WE ALL SHARE
AN INSPIRED RESPONSE IN ALL RELIGIONS;

WE REACH OUT TO EACH OTHER IN TRUST
AND RESPECT COMING CLOSER IN LOVE
AS WE ARE DRAWN TO THE SOURCE OF TRUTH!

The Declaration of Thanksgiving in 1989 stated: "We ... thank the Lord of yesterday and today, but also of tomorrow. Let us be thankful for the tomorrows of this world and all worlds. May this be our true act of thanksgiving." The 1991 statement affirms, "We are sustained through the faith we share."

Among those signing the 1982 statement were: Cynthia C. Wedel of the World Council of Churches; Olof Sundby, Primate of Sweden and Archbishop of Uppsala; the Dalai Lama; and Muzammil Siddiqi of the Islamic Center in Washington, D.C. The 1989 document signers included: Herbert Chilstrom, Bishop of the Evangelical Lutheran Church in America; Diana Eck, Harvard University; Seigen Yamaoka, Bishop of the Buddhist Churches in America; and Juliet Hollister, founder of the Temple of Understanding.

To whose god are they giving thanks and in which faith are they sustained? Are they all worshiping the same god? Is it biblically acceptable for Christians to join people of other religions in a prayer to many gods? Do the Christian leaders associated with Thanksgiving Square believe that the God and Father of our Lord Jesus Christ has gone into partnership with the pagan gods? What ever happened to the first and second Commandments?

Another piece of literature produced by the Thanksgiving Commission offers the following quotes and prayers:

STONE AGE HUNTER: "Our mother, by your kindness, we have found. Without it we receive nothing. We offer you many thanks." — Chenchu tribe of Southern India.

HINDU: "To the Divine Power, who is in the form of action, reverence, and again reverence." — Fifth Mahatmya of Candi.

BUDDHIST: "A noble person is thankful and mindful of the favors he receives from others." — the Buddha.

Many of the people associated with Thanksgiving Square are also involved with the Parliament of World Religions and other New Age organizations. The National Thanksgiving Commission and the Parliament of World Religions listed the endorsement of Sir John Templeton, whose foundation gives the lucrative and syncretistic Templeton Award to various world-religion leaders for "progress in religion."

Robert Muller, who spoke to the Parliament of World Religions, writes about Thanksgiving Square in his book *The New Genesis, Shaping A Global Spirituality:*

> In this beautiful square in Dallas, a new movement has begun ... this world center (Thanksgiving Square) must become a world movement, a spiral of the heart and of the soul outreaching for all leaders, educators, media, world servers and people, reminding them above all we must be grateful to You for what we have received.[27]

EVANGELICALS ON THE PATH TO GLOBAL RELIGION

The presence of evangelicals at the Parliament of World Religions came as a surprise to many, but in recent years influential evangelical leaders have been involved in ecumenical and global religious activities. The World Council of Churches, the National Council of Churches and Thanksgiving Square are gaining support from evangelicals. So-called evangelical feminists are promoting the feminist agenda in their churches.

World Goodwill Newsletter, published by Lucis (formerly Lucifer) Press, one of the largest New Age organizations in existence, has praised the efforts of the Bi-millennial Global Interaction Network (BEGIN), an evangelical organization which is promoting a global celebration of the year 2000. Headed by Jay E. Gary, the Bi-millennial Global Interaction Network has joined with globalist and New Age leaders to observe the year 2000 as a "Year of World Thanksgiving." The United Nations, Thanksgiving Square, New Age organizations, the U.S. Congress, mainline churches and compromising evangelicals will all participate in the global Thanksgiving parade.

Gary stated in the Goodwill Newsletter:

> One common project we are developing is an "International Year of Thanksgiving" in 2000, especially through the United Nations. Dr. Robert Muller has given leadership to this proposal. If any of your readers would like to bring definition to a World Thanks-

giving Year in 2000, marked by reflection, reconciliation, and gratitude between nations, cultures, and peoples, please have them correspond with us. We are collecting articles and papers on these themes for an upcoming *Let's Talk 2000 Forum.* [28]

Jay E. Gary was identified in a bulletin published by BEGIN, as the "author of *The Countdown Has Begun,* Congress planner with the Lausanne Movement, Communication consultant with New Life 2000 (a program of Campus Crusade for Christ), and Designer of the popular "Perspectives" program." Gary's newsletter stated:

IT'S TIME TO GET READY FOR CELEBRATION 2000. For centuries seers and sages have been transfixed on the year 2000. More recently, trend watchers, planners and futurists have hooked their sights to this guiding star. AD 2000, the year itself has been a powerful archetypal symbol for the "millennium"– the end of history and the beginning of a global civilization of peace and prosperity. Whatever the year 2000 brings, it will surely be a once-in-a-lifetime experience. Some have already begun to market the year 2000 with glitzy merchandizing and media bash fit to welcome the biggest New Year's Eve in a thousand years ... Those from the fields of media, education, environment, business, technology and religion should also take part in preparing to celebrate the year 2000 in thought as well as action.[29]

Jay Gary lists globalist, New Age leader Dr. Robert Muller as one of the "key people" in BEGIN's efforts to promote the year 2000. His newsletter also promoted Muller's book *The Birth of the Global Civilization* and highlighted the Parliament of World Religions.[30] Why would any evangelical turn to the United Nations or New Age organizations for help in promoting the year 2000?

Some evangelical leaders and pastors are now promoting a theological view that Christ will come to set up His Kingdom only after Christian influence has swept the world. This view is a perfect match for globalist concepts of world unity through religion and government. Thanksgiving Square and promotions of the year 2000 are attractive to evangelicals who want to usher in the Lord's millennial reign. Because they believe the end justifies the means, these evangelicals see nothing wrong with cooperating with the globalists to bring it about.

Sadly, countless evangelicals are being deceived and drawn into the globalist program. Between now and the year 2000, we will witness compromising evangelical leaders, organizations and churches cruising on the globalists' ecumenical ship of Thanksgiving. Little do they realize their unionistic cruise will make the Titanic look like a Sunday afternoon pleasure trip. Bible-believing Christians whose leaders are promoting unionistic fellowship with New Age and globalist organizations should head for the lifeboats.

EVANGELICALS AND CATHOLICS TOGETHER

Several evangelical leaders have joined with representatives of the Roman Catholic Church in drafting a declaration of agreement, "Evangelicals and Catholics Together: The Christian Mission in the Third Millennium." Evangelicals involved in this venture include Charles Colson of the Prison Fellowship and Pat Robertson of the 700 Club. In addition to pledging themselves to the "common faith" that binds evangelicals and Roman Catholics, the supporters of the declaration agreed that they should no longer seek to proselytize one another's flocks, especially active members.[31]

Leadership for this nonbinding but historical agreement between the Roman Catholic Church and the evangelicals was given by Charles Colson and Roman Catholic priest, Richard John Neuhaus. This represents another trek which Colson has made into the broad ecumenical arena in recent times. In 1993, Colson accepted the Templeton Prize for Progress in Religion at a syncretistic worship service that was planned to coincide with the Parliament of World Religions in Chicago. At the service where Colson acknowledged the award, a Moslem gave the opening prayer and a Buddhist offered the closing prayer.

Richard John Neuhaus, a former pastor in the Lutheran Church-Missouri Synod and later in the Evangelical Lutheran Church in America, converted to Roman Catholicism and was ordained a priest in 1990. Michael Novak, a Roman Catholic and recipient of the 1994 Templeton Prize for Progress in Religion, was also part of the consultation which drafted the document.[32] It seems more than a little coincidental that the last two winners of the syncretistic Templeton Award would be in the vanguard of a Roman Catholic and evangelical agreement.

R.C. Sproul of Ligonier Ministries stated, "I'm afraid the document trivializes the Reformation," suggesting that the evangelicals may have negotiated away justification, "what Luther called the article upon which the church stands or falls." Sproul also commented that the document's section on Scripture was "lacking."[33]

Dave Hunt called the joint declaration the "most significant event in almost 500 years of church history," and "the most devastating blow against the gospel in at least 1000 years." Hunt remarked:

> Amazingly, the document claims that all Catholics are Christians, hold the same faith as evangelicals, and are our "brothers and sisters in Christ." If so, then the Reformation was a tragic mistake which we must all denounce. On this sad juncture in church history, the last words of Hugh Latimer ring in our conscience. Bound back-to-back to the stake with Nicholas Ridley, Latimer, England's most effective gospel preacher at that time, was heard to exclaim as the flames engulfed them, "Be of good comfort, Master Ridley, and play the man. We shall this day, by God's grace, light such a candle in England as I pray shall never be put out." How incredible that the last spark of that Reformation "candle" is now being extinguished by evangelical leaders who owe so much to the very faithfulness of such martyrs! [34]

It is beyond comprehension why Bible-believing evangelicals would enter into such an agreement with the Roman Catholic Church based on two facts: 1) The Roman Catholic Church has not rescinded one doctrine which brought about the Protestant Reformation in 1517. The Roman Catholic Church still denies the doctrine of justification by grace through faith alone; they affirm the doctrines of purgatory, indulgences, masses for the dead, the infallibility of the Pope, and they still believe that Christians need the intercessions of Mary and the saints. 2) To suggest that the Protestant church should not seek the conversion of Roman Catholics is an affront to the clear teachings of the Bible that direct us to witness to all people everywhere who stand in need of salvation. Let the signers of this agreement try to take their message of nonconversion to South America and other Roman Catholic nations of the world where many Roman Catholics mingle spiritism and voodoo with Christianity. Bible-believing missionaries in these countries have committed their lives to bringing people to true faith in Jesus Christ.

Colson indicated that the agreement does not preclude either Roman Catholics or evangelicals from bringing someone to Christ, but it does preclude going after each other's active members. However, church membership is not equal with salvation. Not all active members of evangelical churches or the Roman Catholic Church are bound for heaven. He also stated that when witnessing, we should not criticize the other's church.[35]

Interestingly, the same week the statement was signed, the Vatican released an official document, *The Interpretation of the Bible in the Church,* in which they viciously attacked those who view the Bible as the inerrant Word of God. While the Vatican theologians singled out Protestant fundamentalists' views in their paper, the doctrine of biblical inerrancy is generally held by evangelicals. Apparently fundamentalists are not included in the Roman Catholic/Evangelical agreement, nor are those evangelicals who believe in biblical inerrancy.

Evangelicals who drafted the agreement stressed that the joint statement declares the Bible to be "infallible." However, the Roman Catholic concept of infallibility has a completely different perspective than that which is taught in the Protestant confessions. The Roman Catholic Church still teaches that church tradition and the Bible are equal in authority. Upon that teaching, they have constructed their doctrines regarding Mary, papal infallibility, indulgences and purgatory, to name but a few. Every one of these teachings stands in contradiction to the biblical doctrines of the Reformation — grace alone, faith alone and Scripture alone. It is clear that spiritual cooperation between Bible-believing evangelicals and a church body that requires belief in all these doctrines to the point of eternal damnation is impossible. The suggestion that Roman Catholic people who may be lost without hope in Jesus Christ should no longer be the objects of Protestant missionary endeavors is a gross violation of the Word of God and a contradiction of the very name "evangelical."

It is time for Bible-believing Christians to put "protest" back in Protestantism. While we deplore words and deeds which promote antagonisms between Protestants and Roman Catholics, it is wrong for evangelicals to take the road back to Rome, and it is wrong for Christians to blindly follow them. True believers need the discernment of the Holy Spirit and the Word of God to know when to say "no" to even the most renowned and respected church leaders. Why are so many evangelical pastors silent on this agreement spearheaded by Colson and Neuhaus? The words of the gospel hymn "Where He Leads Me I Will Follow" refer to Jesus Christ, not to misguided leaders.

These observations are not made against Roman Catholic people, nor is my opposition to this agreement an attack upon the Roman Catholic Church. I am simply stating that the Reformation and the issues which brought it about are still a reality that cannot be ignored. The Roman Catholic Church may hold any belief or opinion it so chooses; however, Roman Catholic officials and evangelical leaders are wrong to promote an agreement which tramples upon the clear teachings of God's Word.

There are many Roman Catholic members who have a deep and abiding faith in Jesus Christ. There are Roman Catholics who are standing for right and opposing evil, in accordance with the Word of God. It is appropriate for evangelicals and Roman Catholics who share the same biblical values regarding abortion, pornography and other social issues to individually work in cooperation to rid them from our communities and nation, but for evangelicals to seek an accord with a church body that professes so many unbiblical teachings as part of its creed is a dangerous road to take. Such covenants imply that these doctrinal differences are insignificant. That is the wrong message to send in these days of interfaith cooperation.

CHRISTIANS ARE FORBIDDEN
TO PARTICIPATE IN IDOLATRY

God spoke through his servant the Apostle Paul:

Wherefore, my dearly beloved, flee from idolatry. I speak as to wise men; judge ye what I say. The cup of blessing which we bless, is it not the communion of the blood of Christ? ... But I say, that the things which the Gentiles sacrifice, they sacrifice to devils, and not to God: and I would not that ye should have fellowship with devils. Ye cannot drink the cup of the Lord, and the cup of devils: ye cannot be partakers of the Lord's table, and of the table of devils. Do we provoke the Lord to jealousy? are we stronger than he? (1 Corinthians 10:14-16; 20-22).

Though there is no more basic teaching in Scripture than this, misguided liberal and evangelical church leaders are rushing to cooperate with world religions and declare their equality with Christianity. What message does their acceptance of pagan religions give to people today, especially youth who are constantly bombarded by cults, the New Age movement, the occult and Eastern religions? What is to prevent young people or adults from seeking out and participating in Eastern religions when their pastors and denominations encourage interfaith participation?

THE INTERFAITH MOVEMENT IS A BETRAYAL OF THE LORD

For nearly two thousand years the Great Commission of Christ to "make disciples of all nations" has prompted the church to send missionaries to the furthermost places of the earth. These missionaries left home, family, wealth and nation to become heralds of glad tidings to peoples dwelling in darkness. Participation in the Parliament of World Religions and the one-world religion movement is an affront to God and every true missionary who ever lived. It is apostasy to teach that pagan religions have common ground with Christianity. All religions do not represent many roads leading to the same place. There is one true and living God and only one Savior who can bring us to Him. Every Christian is directed by the Lord of the church to walk in love and consideration for all men. Hate and strife are forbidden. However, that does not mean that we are to accept what the pagans teach or participate with them in worshiping false gods. To the contrary, we are commanded to witness to them the gospel of Christ that they might be saved.

If there is salvation in other than Jesus Christ, or if there is another way of salvation beyond the blood of Christ poured out on the cross, then God owes Jesus an apology for unanswered prayer in the Garden of Gethsemane and us an explanation. Jesus declared in John 14:6: "... I am the way, the truth, and the life: no man cometh unto the Father, but by Me." Jesus proclaimed in John 11:25 and 26: "... I am the resurrection, and the life: he that believeth in me, though he were dead, yet shall he live: And whosoever liveth and believeth in me shall never die." Jesus is either everything He claimed, or He is the greatest fraud ever perpetrated on the world!

Paul said: "And if Christ be not raised, your faith is vain; ye are yet in your sins" (1 Corinthians 15:17). But we know by grace through faith that Jesus Christ is the risen-again, divine Son of God, and the only Savior of the world. We have confidence that all the Bible teaches is true. We cannot, we must not, deny our Lord and Savior in this age of apostasy and compromise.

COME OUT FROM AMONG THEM

In this decade we are witnessing the binding of the apostate church with world religions. Christians in liberal churches are witnessing a sell-out of the gospel of Jesus Christ through their denomination's participation in the one-world religion movement. Church members who are being told that cooperation with other religions is for "humanitarian purposes" and "for world peace" are being deceived. Cooperation with other religions is idolatry. Christians who participate in this betrayal of the Lord or tolerate syncretism (blending of false religions with Christianity) will be required to give an account on Judgment Day.

The participation of Christian churches in the interfaith movement is one of the greatest violations of God's Word that I have witnessed in my lifetime. This departure makes most others pale by comparison. I state as plainly as I can, building what I say upon the Word of God: The participation of Christian churches in the one-world religion movement will not stand! It is an evil so perverse that God will not allow it to go unanswered. In the history of Christianity, was there ever a greater example of the church's fall from truth? Was there ever a greater illustration of the church's desperate need for revival?

Bible-believing Christians should cease their participation in congregations that are involved in any of the one-world religion organizations, either directly or indirectly through their denominational affiliation. Contending for the faith on this issue means separation as well as opposition. Jesus Christ is coming again. He is coming, not for a harlot church wallowing in apostasy, but for His holy spotless Bride whom He has redeemed with His precious Blood.

RISE YE CHILDREN OF SALVATION

Rise ye children of salvation,
    all who cleave to Christ the Head;
Wake, awake, O mighty nation,
    ere the foe on Zion tread;
He draws nigh, and would defy
    all the hosts of God most high.

Saints and martyrs long before us
    firmly on this ground have stood;
See their banner waving o'er us,
    conquerors through the Savior's Blood.
Ground we hold, whereon of old
    fought the faithful and the bold.

Fighting, we shall be victorious
    by the Blood of Christ our Lord;
On our foreheads, bright and glorious,
    shines the witness of His Word;
Spear and shield on battlefield,
    His great Name we cannot yield.

When his servants stand before him
    each receiving his reward,
When his saints in light adore Him,
    giving glory to the Lord;
'Victory!' our song shall be
    like the thunder of the sea.

Justus Falckner, 1672-1723

Chapter 9

Contending for the Faith — Against the One-World Government

And I stood upon the sand of the sea, and saw a beast rise up out of the sea, having seven heads and ten horns, and upon his horns ten crowns, and upon his heads the name of blasphemy. And the beast which I saw was like unto a leopard, and his feet were as the feet of a bear, and his mouth as the mouth of a lion: and the dragon gave him his power, and his seat, and great authority (Revelation 13:1,2).

A one-world government is an idea whose time has come, according to many political and religious leaders. Norman Cousins, honorary chairman of Planetary Citizens, president of the World Federalist Association, a member of the Council on Foreign Relations and the Trilateral Commission, has stated: "World government is coming, in fact it is inevitable. No arguments for or against it can change that fact."[1]

Those who warn of current plans to implement global systems of government and religion are often accused of conducting scare campaigns, but mounting evidence is becoming harder to ignore. It is difficult to imagine the United States or other great Western powers surrendering national sovereignty or divesting economic control over their own destinies, but that is exacting what is unfolding. The world planners who hold positions of influence in governments around the world are legion. While America sleeps, the globalists gather to plan their strategy for the New World Order which will be supported by a global economic system and a unified military.

Efforts to create world government have been quietly developing for decades. H. G. Wells described such a global community in graphic detail in his book *The New World Order*, published in 1939. Its implementation is being brought about piecemeal through treaties, trade agreements, disarmament plans, and unified military operations. The principal components being used to orchestrate public acceptance of a one-world government are economics (including a redistribution of wealth), environmental concerns and world peace-keeping operations. The Humanist Manifesto II, drafted and signed in 1973, states:

> We deplore the division of humankind on nationalistic grounds. We have reached a turning point in human history where the best option is to transcend the limits of national sovereignty and to move toward the building of a world community ... a system of world law and world order based upon transnational federal government.

What appear as isolated events may seem benign at first glance, but when they are viewed together, the big picture of a unified world begins to emerge. The North American Trade Agreement (NAFTA), the General Agreement on Trade and Tariffs (GATT), the Common Market of Europe (now called the European Community) with its unified monetary system, and trade agreements in Asia — all are helping to shape the global economy. If the sovereign nations of Europe are able to achieve a common currency, can a world currency be far behind? Peace-keeping operations by the United Nations and its growing military influence are stepping stones to a global army or police force.

Major players in the promotion of global government include the United Nations, the Council on Foreign Relations, the Trilateral Commission and the World Federalists. New Age organizations, many associated with world religions, also carry the banner for world government. Conferences relating to three deliberately contrived global issues — economics, environment and peace — frequently grab the headlines, but only the discerning understand their true agenda. Speakers and participants at these conferences invariably come from the groups previously mentioned, as well as other global and New Age organizations.

It is not possible in this brief chapter to detail all of the world leaders and global organizations, both secular and religious, that are now engaged in this nefarious enterprise, but an overview of this subject should leave no doubt as to their plans to bring about a world system of government. Regardless of anyone's prophetical views concerning the coming antichrist or a global government, the facts regarding its implementation in our time can no longer be dismissed. Christians need to become informed about the significance of world events that are now unfolding.

Why should the implementation of a one-world government concern the Christian community? Are not global peace, the eradication of poverty and a pollution-free environment worthy objectives for all humanity? If world government is the only means to achieve these goals, is it not worth the price?

First of all, Christians need to understand that the planned world government will be a godless structure. Its utopian promises are an illusion. The lion will not lie down with the lamb when the antichrist is in power. Though he masquerades as "the Prince of Peace," any peace produced by the antichrist will be achieved through tyrannical power and force. The world may experience a measure of peace under the New World Order for a brief period of time, but according to the Scriptures world peace will be shattered. "For when they shall say, Peace and safety; then sudden destruction cometh upon them, as travail upon a woman with child; and they shall not escape" (1 Thessalonians 5:3).

Secondly, the coming world government will be founded on secular humanistic principles and will consider biblical values to be counter-productive to the New World Order. The global government, built upon the shifting sands of ethical relativism, will oppose moral absolutes.

Finally, the coming world government will systematically destroy its opposition. Those who will not "worship the golden image" of world government and bear its mark will pay a terrible price. The one-world religion and the one-world government now appearing on the scene will represent the ultimate test for Christians who "earnestly contend for the faith." The coming world government will be aligned with the emerging world religion which will appear to be "Christian" or compatible with Christianity. Its rhetoric will deceive most church people.

THE TESTIMONY OF WORLD LEADERS

As recently as 1992, the number two man in the Clinton State Department, Strobe Talbott, was quoted as saying:

All countries are basically social arrangements ... No matter how permanent and even sacred they may seem at any one time, in fact they are all artificial and temporary ... Perhaps national sovereignty wasn't such a great idea after all ... But it has taken the events in our own wondrous and terrible century to clinch the case for world government.[2]

Talbott is a member of the Council on Foreign Relations and the Trilateral Commission. He and Bill Clinton, both Rhodes scholars, were roommates at Oxford University.[3]

Richard Gardner, another member of the Clinton administration and former U.S. deputy assistant secretary of state, wrote in the CFR's *Foreign Affairs*, April 1974: "An end run around national sovereignty, eroding it piece by piece, is likely to get us to world order faster than the old-fashioned frontal attack."[4]

Boutros Boutros-Ghali, Secretary-General of the United Nations, has advocated the formation of a permanent UN army and wants the UN to be authorized as a taxing authority. Can you imagine a universal draft which requires our young men and women to serve under the UN flag? Or a separate tax bill on April 15 designated for the United Nations? These are the aspirations of influential globalists now in power.

Mikhail Gorbachev, former head of the Soviet Union who now heads the global Green Cross organization, called for "giving the United Nations expanded authority to regulate military conflicts, economic relations, environmental protection and ... also called for enhancing the power of the afflicted International Court of Justice to decide international disputes."[5]

President George Bush, on October 1, 1990, urged the United Nations General Assembly "to press forward to cap a historic movement toward a new world order." Then he concluded:

And so let it be said of the final decade of the twentieth century, this was a time when humankind came into its own ... to bring about a revolution of the spirit and the mind and began a journey into a new day, a new age, and a new partnership of nations. The U.N. is now fulfilling its promise as the world's parliament of peace.[6]

In recent years, we have witnessed the increasing power of the United Nations in military affairs. The Persian Gulf War was a classic example of military might under the control of the New World Order. Little by little, the United States is turning over military authority to the United Nations. Speaking to the United Nations General Assembly on September 21, 1991, President Bush stated:

I welcome the Secretary General's call for a new agenda to strengthen the United Nations' ability to prevent, contain and resolve conflict across the globe ... Robust peace-keeping requires men and equipment that only member states can provide ... These forces must be available on short notice at the request of the Security Council ... The United States is prepared to make available our bases and facilities for multinational training and field exercises. One such base, nearby, with facilities is Fort Dix.[7]

D.L. Cuddy, in his book *Now Is The Dawning Of The New Age New World Order,* quotes excerpts from Howard Phillips' address to conservative leaders in Washington, D.C. on April 13, 1991. His analysis and warning regarding the venture of the U.S. into the global system should be shouted from the housetops.

The New World Order constitutes no proper part of the heritage of American liberty. ... Today, America's autonomy and independence are profoundly challenged — not by the armies of foreign tyrants or even the intrigues of domestic enemies, but by the immense power of forces which seek openly to diminish or abolish our distinctiveness as a free nation. Their perverted idealism is based on a secular humanist vision of "one world"— a Utopian world unified by the abolition of borders, conflicts, and the enforced disregard of distinctions in character, heritage, and faith. ... Submitting to a New World Order requires that America eventually surrender its independence, its unique political institutions and laws, and even the control of its own foreign policy to institutions and individuals beyond accountability, in which governing bodies bear no direct relation to the people from whose consent their legitimacy is properly derived. ... The New World Order is not a new idea. It has long been a dream of Utopian humanists and of commercial activists who seek to break down political entities which are inconvenient to their pursuit of profits.[8]

THE DECLARATION OF INTERDEPENDENCE

Globalists are now calling for the adoption of a world constitution that will be framed as part of the United Nations and supersede nation-state constitutions. A Declaration of Interdependence, prepared during the 1976 bicentennial celebrations by the World Affairs Council of Philadelphia, and signed by 131 members of the United States Congress, states:

> Two centuries ago our forefathers brought forth a new nation; now we must join with others to bring forth a new world order. ... Narrow notions of national sovereignty must not be permitted to curtail that obligation. ... We affirm that a world without law is a world without order, and we call upon all nations to strengthen and to sustain the United Nations and its specialized agencies, and other institutions of world order, and to broaden the jurisdiction of the World Court, that these may preside over a reign of law that will not only end wars but end as well that mindless violence which terrorizes our society even in times of peace.[9]

D.L. Cuddy observed that Congresswoman Marjorie Holt refused to sign the Declaration, saying:

> It calls for the surrender of our national sovereignty to international organizations. It declares that our economy should be regulated by international authorities. It proposes that we enter a "new world order" that would redistribute the wealth created by the American people.[10]

THE COUNCIL ON FOREIGN RELATIONS (CFR)

The Council on Foreign Relations, founded in 1921, can trace its early beginnings to the Institute of International Affairs. The Institute of International Affairs came about in the early part of the present century through financing from the Rhodes Trust. Cecil Rhodes, an Englishman, believed in world government to such an extent that he established a secret society to promote it. Rhodes scholars are funded through the Rhodes Trust. D. L. Cuddy has made the following observations regarding Rhodes:

> The Rhodes scholarships were named after Cecil Rhodes, and according to Rhodes biographer, Sarah Millin: "The government of the world was Rhodes' simple desire." According to (President)

Clinton's mentor, Prof. Carroll Quigley at Georgetown University: "The (Rhodes) scholarships were merely a facade to conceal the secret society, or, more accurately, they were to be one of the instruments by which members of the secret society could carry out Rhodes' purpose."

Quigley related in *Tragedy and Hope* (1966) that Rhodes' plan stated in 1890 for his scholarships was that after 30 years there would be "between two and three thousand men in the prime of life scattered all over the world, each one of whom, moreover, would have been specially — mathematically — selected towards the Founder's purposes." This would have been around 1920, the time of the founding of the Council on Foreign Relations (CFR), which Quigley indicated was part of Rhodes' plan and said, "The board of the CFR have carried ever since the marks of their origin."[11]

The Council on Foreign Relations has helped to organize other global organizations, including the World Federalists Association and the Trilateral Commission. It was the CFR's influence which brought about the establishment of the United Nations following World War II. The CFR is funded by some of the world's richest families and members of the international banking community. World economics play a primary role in the objectives of the CFR.

Membership in the CFR is by invitation. Their roster is composed of some of the most powerful and influential people in American politics, including President Bill Clinton. Numerous high-level positions in the Clinton administration are held by members of the Council on Foreign Relations, starting with Secretary of State, Warren Christopher. Membership in the CFR seems to be a prerequisite for gaining top positions in the United States government. Fifteen of the last 20 men who served as Secretary of State were members of the CFR. Most Presidents dating back to Franklin D. Roosevelt (Eisenhower, Kennedy, Nixon, Ford, Carter, Bush, Clinton) and their ranking administrative staff members have been members of the CFR. John F. Kennedy's administration was filled with CFR people. James W. Wardner, in his informative article "The Planned Destruction of America," offers a most perceptive quote by John Kenneth Galbraith, a member of the Kennedy team and a member of the CFR. Galbraith stated: "Those of us who had worked for the Kennedy election were tolerated in the government for that reason and had a say, but foreign policy was still with the Council on Foreign Relations people."[12]

Foreign Affairs, a journal of the Council on Foreign Relations, is one of the most influential publications in the world according to *Time* magazine. Its articles regularly promote world federalism. James W. Wardner quotes from an article in *Foreign Affairs* by Richard Cooper, a former under-secretary of state during the Carter administration, in which the author offers a plan for a one-world currency and a one-world bank: "I suggest a radical alternative scheme ... the creation of a common currency for all the industrial democracies, with a common monetary policy and a joint Bank of Issue to determine that monetary policy."[13]

Rear Admiral Chester Ward who was part of the Council on Foreign Relations for 16 years resigned because of their desire "to bring about the surrender of the national sovereignty and the national independence of the United States." He wrote:

Once the ruling members of the CFR have decided that the U.S. government should adopt a particular policy, the very substantial research facilities of the CFR are put to work to develop arguments, intellectual and emotional, to support the new policy, and to confound and discredit, intellectually and politically, any opposition.[14]

THE TRILATERAL COMMISSION

The Trilateral Commission was formulated in 1972 under the direction of David Rockefeller, chairman of the Council on Foreign Relations and chairman of Chase Manhattan Bank. It was formally established in 1983 through the leadership of Zbigniew Brzezinski, President Carter's national security adviser. The Trilateral Commission has three major goals — a one world economy, a one-world government, and a one-world religion. Membership in the organization comes from North America, Europe and Japan — regions which control the vast riches of the world. Trade agreements with China and Vietnam, as well as NAFTA and Asia/Pacific trade agreements, were engineered by the Trilateralists. James W. Warner further described the agenda of the Trilateral Commission:

The Trilateralists have kindly "volunteered" to take the lead in "coping with pressing problems and shaping emerging conditions."

They seek an age of post-nationalism when, devoid of ethnic culture and history, the social, economic and political values esteemed by the Trilateral "volunteers" will be transformed into universal values. That is, a universal economy, a universal government (appointed, not elected), and a universal faith. Likeminded government officials and business leaders are to carry out national and international policy formation. There must be "more technical focus and lesser public awareness." This lessens the chance for people to grasp the overall scheme of the world managers and organize serious resistance.[15]

Barry Goldwater described the Trilateral Commission this way: "In my view, the Trilateral Commission represents a skillful, coordinated effort to seize control and consolidate the four centers of power: political, monetary, intellectual, and ecclesiastical."[16] Goldwater also stated: "What the Trilaterals truly intend is the creation of a worldwide economic power superior to the political government of the nation-states involved. As managers and creators of the system, they will rule the world."[17]

THE ONE-WORLD ECONOMY

"Don't leave home without it" signals not only the modern revolution in personal credit, but also its global usefulness. A traveler from Butte, Montana, can now make purchases in Hong Kong by check or credit card and never need to exchange currency or use cash. A giant computer in Brussels records and clears global transactions in seconds.

Some refer to this as a cashless society. Social Security and payroll payments can be made directly to individual bank accounts. Bills can be paid automatically from those same accounts, requiring neither cash or checks to transact business. These unique financial arrangements are more than mere convenience; they are the technology required for a global monetary system. Technology now exists to record individual credit history and thousands of personal details on a tiny microchip.

Some have suggested placing this chip under the skin so that the information can be protected. It could be retrieved instantaneously at stores, hospitals, police stations, banks or wherever needed. Such a system would make credit cards obsolete.

Stock market reports from all over the world are broadcast daily by financial news programs. The world markets are already tied together as investors from one nation trade the securities of another. Energy and precious metals are priced globally. Interest rates in Germany, England, Japan and the United States impact one another's economies. While nations still control many of their financial interests, those decisions are being eroded through international trade and monetary agreements.

Boutros-Ghali's call for a Peace Fund and power to raise revenues for the United Nations received support from the Carnegie Endowment's National Commission on America and the New World. The report stated: "Any plausible vision for America's future role in the world must include a renewed financial commitment to the United Nations."[18] Suggestions for U.N. revenue raising include a tax on international air travel, a tax on gasoline and other energy products, and VAT taxes on goods crossing international borders.

A world currency and credit system will require a central banking system to determine financial policy, as well as authorization to print money. That mechanism is already in place through the International Monetary Fund and the World Bank, established at the end of World War II. Richard N. Cooper, in his article published in *Foreign Affairs,* Fall 1984, proposed "A Monetary System For the Future." Cooper stated:

> The key point is that monetary control — the issuance of currency and of reserve credit — would be in the hands of the new Bank of Issue, not in the hands of any national government. ...This one-currency regime is much too radical to envisage in the near future. But it is not too radical to envisage 25 years from now ... It will require many years of consideration before people become accustomed to the idea.[19]

The Club of Rome's 200 members also want to see the establishment of a global economy that shares the wealth, because they maintain "the system of market economy countries based on competition is motivated by self interest and ultimately on greed."[20]

ENVIRONMENTAL ISSUES

A centerpiece in the world environmental program is Green Cross, headed by former Soviet leader, Mikhail Gorbachev. The parent organization for Green Cross is the Global Forum of Spiritual and Parliamentary Leaders on Human Survival. "Founded in 1985, the Forum provides an interfaith meeting ground for doomsday scientists, utopian politicians and spiritual leaders from the world's major religions."[21]

Every conceivable environmental problem from acid rain to global warming is being touted as justification for global cooperation and, ultimately, world government. The United Nations Earth Summit, held in Rio de Janeiro in 1993, was global, pagan and New Age. Speakers included Vice-President Al Gore (author of *Earth in the Balance*), Fidel Castro, Mikhail Gorbachev, and Lester Brown of the World Watch Institute.

CHILDREN ARE BEING TRAINED TO LIVE IN THE NEW WORLD ORDER

Politically correct concepts now being promoted by politicians and religious leaders portray life in the New World Order. Children in public schools are being systematically trained to become world citizens, conforming to the one-world philosophy and politically correct thought. Curricula in public schools are designed to achieve this goal. Outcome Based Education, now being imposed in many school districts across the nation, has little regard for academic achievement. Instead, it endeavors to mold young minds to accept the one-world view of life as well as the moral standards established by a secular society.

A course of study currently being taught in hundreds of public schools in the United States is entitled *Living With Our Deepest Differences: Religious Liberty in a Pluralistic Society.* The course, produced by the First Liberty Institute in Fairfax, Virginia, and written by Charles C. Haynes, president of the National Council on Religion and Public Education, has the endorsement of the most liberal educational organizations in the country, including the National Education Association.

Furthermore, it is supported by the National Council of Churches and the National Association of Evangelicals. How the National Association of Evangelicals could have been persuaded to endorse this New Age educational program is a mystery. A modest amount of research reveals that First Liberty Institute, a coalition of education and religious groups, is networked with the Temple of Understanding and many other New Age groups. The Temple of Understanding and the Hartley Film Foundation supply New Age, interfaith films for schools that are offering the course.

Environmental issues and events, including Earth Day, are another way the New Age movement is molding the minds of our children. D. L. Cuddy, in his book *Now Is The Dawning Of The New Age New World Order*, quotes from an article originally carried in the Minneapolis *Star Tribune*. It read:

> Mary Jane Rachner explained that "today in the Minneapolis schools, the liberal elite stands guard. When I served as a substitute teacher in the third grade room and announced to the children that we would begin the day with the pledge to the flag, a teacher who apparently had been listening outside the door stepped in and told me that saying the pledge was not customary in the Putnam School. She said the custom was to pledge allegiance to the Earth, and she pointed to where the Earth-worshippers' pledge was posted on the wall. ... One of the children asked the teacher, 'Can't we do the pledge to the flag if we want to?' A stern look was the reply."[22]

THE GLOBAL THREAT TO CHRISTIANS

It is difficult to assess all the challenges that the New World Order will pose for Bible-believing Christians. But what is unfolding today in the areas of education, economics, social morality, abortion, euthanasia, homosexuality, interfaith activity and increased governmental control over our private lives is a portent of things to come. It is clear that many compromises will be required by Christians if persecution is to be avoided. Clearly, the vast majority of church people will take that route.

More and more, people are clamoring for the government to do something about crime, health issues and economic security. As the crime rate increases, causing citizens to feel threatened in their own homes, they will eagerly surrender personal freedoms for security. When the world economy goes into a tailspin, as it will, people will demand a solution, even if that solution means the surrender of once-treasured national interests. When the illusion of world peace is shattered, as it will be shattered, cries will go up around the world for stronger international controls on tyrants and belligerent nations. It is possible that the world planners will orchestrate many of these economic and military catastrophes to hasten their objective of world government. Wars and economic woes have been orchestrated by lesser motives for centuries.

THE PARTNERSHIP OF GOVERNMENT AND RELIGION

George W. Blount, a Methodist clergyman, began his book *Peace Through World Government* with these words:

> Three facts in the present human scene make World Government possible. These are the Christian religion, the United States, and World Federalists, U.S.A. These three, working together, can and will create World Government in due time. ... The Christian religion furnishes the inspiration, and the goal, essential for the achievement of world peace through World Government.[23]

The Methodist clegyman stated the case for the involvement of the whole Christian church, as well as his own denomination in the establishment of a world government.

> The Church needs a definite instrument with which to work in this field. The Church must have an effective instrument through which to channel its truth and moral motivation ... That instrument is at hand. It is now in existence. It is the World Association of World Federalists, U.S.A. ... The Christian Church should therefore, give full and complete support to, and adequate cooperation with World Federalist, U.S.A., for the achievement of lasting peace between nations. ... Our hope is that the United Methodist Church, a major Protestant Denomination, will lead the way.[24]

While many might dismiss Blount's comments as merely one man's opinion, they represent both the argument and the clarion call for the end-time church to become leagued with the one-world government. It is my belief that the one-world religion will wrap a blanket of approval around all ventures which promote global harmony. Any attempts to promote moral absolutes or religious exclusivism — such as the doctrine of salvation through Jesus Christ alone — will be construed as being out of step with the new "inclusivism" and vigorously opposed. Deviant sexual behavior will be legitimatized through law, with the sanction of the apostate church; writing or speaking against it will likely result in lawsuits and arrests. Churches and Christian ministries that oppose homosexuality may lose their tax exempt status.

World government and world religion will be ushered in on the wings of political expediency. Their gradual formation will gain worldwide support as the global issues of economics and world peace become critical to all nations. It will make sense to most inhabitants of the earth. Opposition will be tantamount to treason.

THE HOPE OF ALL BELIEVERS

I firmly believe that we are living in the last days. Jesus Christ is coming soon. Christians may be required to face many trials before His coming as our forefathers faced before us, but He who called us is faithful. We are summoned as followers of Christ to "be faithful unto death" and He will "give us a crown of life." Paul gave us the right focus:

> But watch thou in all things, endure afflictions, do the work of an evangelist, make full proof of thy ministry. For I am now ready to be offered, and the time of my departure is at hand. I have fought a good fight, I have finished my course, I have kept the faith: Henceforth there is laid up for me a crown of righteousness, which the Lord, the righteous judge, shall give me at that day: and not to me only, but unto all them also that love his appearing (2 Timothy 4:5-8).

> May God help us all to be faithful!

LIFT UP YOUR HEADS

Lift up your heads, ye gates of brass,
   ye bars of iron yield,

And let the King of Glory pass,
   the Cross is in the field;

That banner, brighter than the star
   that leads the train of night,

Shines on their march, and guides from far
   His servants to the fight.

A holy war those servants wage;
   in that mysterious strife,

The powers of heaven and hell
   engage for more than death or life.

Ye armies of the living God,
   ye warriors of Christ's host,

Where hallowed footsteps never trod,
   take your appointed post.

Though few and small and weak your hands,
   strong in your Captain's strength

Go to the conquest of all the lands;
   all must be his at length.

Uplifted are the gates of brass,
   the bars of iron yield;

Behold the King of Glory pass:
   The Cross hath won the field.

James Montgomery, 1771-1854

147

Chapter 10

Contending for the Faith — Against the Feminist Onslaught

There is neither Jew nor Greek, there is neither bond nor free, there is neither male nor female: for ye are all one in Christ Jesus ... (Galatians 3:28).

I beseech Euodias, and beseech Syntyche, that they be of the same mind in the Lord. And I entreat thee also, true yoke-fellow, help those women which laboured with me in the gospel, with Clement also, and with other my fellow-labourers, whose names are in the book of life (Philippians 4:2,3).

Men and women of all races and tongues, rich and poor, educated and illiterate, powerful and weak — all are sinners in need of a Savior. "For all have sinned, and come short of the glory of God" (Romans 3:23). The ground is level at the cross. Christ died for all, from Adam and Eve to the last person to be born, so that "whosoever will may come." The message of faith and repentance proclaimed by Peter in the streets of Jerusalem has not changed: "Neither is there salvation in any other: for there is none other name under heaven given among men, whereby we must be saved" (Acts 4:12). That is the gospel of Jesus Christ, pure and plain.

Women and men are portrayed in the Bible with all their virtues and flaws. The Scriptures are filled with accounts of godly women whose lives serve as an example to us all. When Jesus walked on earth He demonstrated love and respect for both men and women. Paul offered words of praise for the women who labored with him in spreading the gospel. Whether in the Old or New Testaments, godly and virtuous women are highly honored. "Who can find a virtuous woman? For her price is far above rubies ... Her children arise up, and call her blessed; her husband also, and he praiseth her " (Proverbs 31:10,28). Those who accuse the Bible of having a male bias which demeans women are

149

wrong. "… God is no respecter of persons:" (Acts 10:34).

Women are accorded every spiritual right and privilege by the Scriptures, for "in Christ there is neither male nor female." Jesus' promises of eternal life were offered without distinction to all men and women who believe in Him. Perhaps the greatest message of hope ever uttered by Jesus was first spoken to a woman: "… I am the resurrection, and the life: he that believeth in me, though he were dead, yet shall he live: And whosoever liveth and believeth in me shall never die …" (John 11:25,26). Women were first to arrive at the empty tomb on Resurrection morning, and a woman was first to see the risen Savior. Women were in the upper room on the day of Pentecost when the Holy Spirit fell on all who were assembled. One day, women and men shall stand together around the throne of God with the angels and archangels in everlasting worship and praise. They will see the Lord face to face and share the same eternal joys. Those who have gone to be with the Lord are seldom identified in the Bible as men or women, but as saints, the redeemed of the Lord, the great multitude, God's servants, the Bride of Christ, and the Church. The charge that God's Word demeans women is heresy.

THE DIVINE ORDER OF CREATION

The unique physical differences which compliment and attract men and women to each other are God-created. All other physical attractions, being unnatural, are contrary to the will of God. The unique physical and spiritual roles which the Lord assigns to men and women are mutually fulfilling. Marriage between men and women is God-ordained. "For this cause shall a man leave his father and mother, and shall be joined unto his wife and they two shall be one flesh" (Ephesians 5:31). Children are a blessing from the Lord (Psalm 127:3). The Creator established the family as the foundation for a stable society. He commanded children to honor and obey their parents. The Lord directed parents to instruct their children in His laws "so that they may be brought up to lead a godly life until the Day of Jesus Christ."[1] Parents are to care for their children when they are young, then be cared for by their children when they are old. This is God's social security program. Husbands are commanded to love their wives "as Christ loved the church," because "… the husband is the head of the wife, even as

150

Christ is the head of the church ..." (Ephesians 5:23,25). Whether the feminists agree or not, this is the divine order of creation.

When the divine order of creation is not honored, or when the roles which God has designed for men and women are not followed, the consequences for society are devastating. Today we are witnessing the tragic results of sin and rebellion inflicted upon church and society by those who defy the Word of God, including those in the feminist movement. From the holocaust in the abortion clinics to the implementation of the homosexual agenda, the feminist scourge threatens to destroy America. The women's liberation movement is more rightly called the women's bondage movement, because it enslaves all who are deceived by it. The human mind could never conceive a plan which frees women and men from the bondage of sin; it is Christ alone, who breaks the chains of sin and death. "If the Son therefore shall make you free, ye shall be free indeed" (John 8:36).

Times may have changed, but the divine pattern of creation remains the same. Times may have changed, but the desperately wicked heart of man has not changed. Man in his sinfulness has oppressed women and denied their basic rights, but neither the Creator nor the Scriptures are to blame.

While the feminist movement has raised some legitimate issues which needed to be addressed in our sinful society, such as abuse, sexual harassment and the treatment of women in the work place, can we truly say that we are better off as a nation? Are we better off when the majority of our children are being raised in day care centers? Are we better off now that less than 30 percent of American homes are composed of traditional families — mother, father, and children? Are we better off with homosexual "couples" adopting children? Are we better off with our 50 percent divorce rate? Are we better off with society's emphasis on materialism, so that women who would prefer to stay at home are forced to work in order to make ends meet? So many of our nation's problems involve the disintegration of the family, and feminism is much to blame.

Was the church wrong to deny women ordination during more than 1900 years of history? Is it just the times that have changed, or have portions of the church relinquished biblical doctrines regarding the roles of women? Sadly, few have bothered to investigate the answers to these questions. Swept along with the rising tide of women's liberation and feminism, many Christians have allowed these issues to go without comment or challenge. Yet no movement in history has brought about so much destruction and upheaval within the church as has feminism.

The destructive nature of the feminist movement is little understood by the Christian community. Their plans and true motivations are often disguised. Church people tend to think women's ordination is the chief issue for feminists in the church when, in fact, it is only the tip of the iceberg. The feminist movement is bringing about a revolution in theology and practice. They intend to remake (re-imagine) the church into their own image, and increasingly they are in the positions to do so. Women now constitute 30 percent of the student enrollment in mainline seminaries, and are approaching 50 percent at several seminaries. Women, many of whom are radical feminists, are filling the pulpits of the nation's churches. The total of women clergy in the United States now exceeds 30,000, and estimates expect that number to double by the year 2000. The United Methodists have more than 4200 female pastors; the Presbyterians are approaching 2500; while the Evangelical Lutheran Church in America has approximately 1500 women pastors.[2] Feminists hold chairs in the religion departments of mainline church colleges and universities, as well as seminaries. They are rewriting the Bible and theology to conform with their humanistic views, and they are introducing perverted sexuality and goddess worship in bizarre liturgical rituals. As one lesbian, feminist clergywoman stated at the RE-Imagining Conference, "Sexuality and spirituality have come together — and Church, we're going to teach you." (The RE-Imagining Conference is described later in this chapter.) This is no trifling issue. The eternal destinies of generations are at stake.

Feminist Rosemary Radford Ruether, Professor of graduate studies at Garrett-Evangelical Theological Seminary, Evanston, Illinois, who has written several books on women's spirituality, stated:

Today, women are in the vanguard of the aborning civilization; and it is to the women that we look for salvation in the healing and restorative waters of Aquarius. It is to such a New Age that we look now with hope as the present age of masculism succeeds in destroying itself ... The rot of masculine materialism has indeed permeated all spheres of twentieth century life.

... the wise woman knows that a resistant humanity is not yet ready for the complete rooting out and removal of traditional Christianity. But subversion and sabotage by women and the men whom they dominate will fix that, to be followed by a new kind of Christianity freed from the bonds of patriarchy and purified of the last vestiges of sexism, clericalism, and militarism.[3]

Rosemary Ruether was invited to present the 1994 Hein-Fry Lecture Series at the seminaries of the Evangelical Lutheran Church in America.

THE APOSTASY OF FEMINIST THEOLOGY

Theological error is damaging; heresy is dangerous; but apostasy seeks the destruction of true Christian faith. Feminists, having gone for the jugular of church doctrine, are apostatizing the faith at every opportunity, insisting that the God of Scriptures must be transformed into a goddess. Feminists in mainline churches refuse to baptize in the Name of the Father, and of the Son, and of the Holy Spirit. Instead, they baptize in the name of the Creator, Lover, and Sustainer, or by some other supposedly non-sexist formula. Roman Catholic Sister Sandra Schneiders, Professor of New Testament studies at The Jesuit School of Theology in Berkeley, California, mockingly referred to the Trinity as "an old man, a young man and a bird."[4] Bible-believing Christians should refuse to worship with anyone who takes liberties with God's Name. God has exalted above all things His Name and His Word (Psalm 138:2). Jesus Christ specifically commanded the church to baptize in the Name of the Father, Son and Holy Spirit (Matthew 28:19).

Feminist theologians (the term is an oxymoron) have openly denied Jesus' atonement and resurrection. They have referred to the doctrine of the atonement as "child abuse," questioning how God the Father could demand the cruel death of a son. At the World Council of Churches' RE-Imagining Conference, the atonement of Christ was viciously attacked by several speakers who received, not rebuke or censure, but thunderous applause.

Others are more subtle in their questioning of Christ's atonement. Rita Nakashima Brock, an associate professor of humanities at Hamline University, St. Paul, Minnesota, stated that the atonement of Christ leaves much out of the human plight:

At the root of atonement is the understanding that we're all bad, and that we don't have the power ourselves to fix the problem. When we depend on one with more power to absolve us, we don't have to fear any consequences of our actions. When we say that Jesus takes on the sins of the world as the door to (personal) salvation, it doesn't get at the fact that a whole lot of innocent people are sinned against by bad people ... It also denies the sense of even good people who get caught up in highly abusive, oppressive systems that cause pain to people.[5]

Brock stated at the WCC's RE-Imagining Conference:

Remember, incarnation is an activity; God is a verb, not a state of being. When we take responsibility we can use our power to love, to nurture, to enable freedom and willfulness of others. Incarnating the love of God. In taking responsibility, we can say the incarnation of God is here and here and here and here working where she is needed, where we are needed. The activity of incarnation is what Audrey Lord called, "erotic power at work."[6]

Mary Ellen Ashcroft, assistant professor of English at Bethel College, Arden Hills, Minnesota, and Holly Bridges Elliott have written a Lenten devotional *Bearing Our Sorrows,* in which they present various and conflicting views of the atonement of Christ. Elliott stated that the book outlines the basic understanding of atonement. "We don't believe God is a displeased deity that's so unhappy with the world that he demands the ultimate payment," she said. Ashcroft went on to comment:

The mystery of the cross can never be reduced to some simple, human thing like God did this to his son. That's so simplistic and inadequate. The cross is inevitably going to be a mystery, and we need many people giving meaning to it in many ways.[7]

Brock also stated:

But the other side of atonement is that God's love is so overwhelmingly gracious that God was willing to die for the sake of all humanity ... that doesn't get at the question of what about people who are sinned against. There needs to be an understanding of liberation, and atonement doesn't do that.

The long-standing fundamental contradiction in Christianity (has been) between affirming love and affirming power, control and dominance. The Christian tradition has slid into power and control too much. If you think carefully about the meaning of love, it cannot coexist with worshiping power, control or dominance. They are a violation of love in a relationship.[8]

THE FEMINIST ASSAULT ON THE SCRIPTURES

What do you do when you want to create a new theology for the church, but the Scriptures stand in the way? Solution — rewrite them! Social feminists endeavor to implement changes using politically correct speech; religious feminists employ non-sexist language, reconstructed theology and the re-imagining of biblical content.

The feminists have many allies in their efforts. The National Council of Churches produced *An Inclusive Language Lectionary* and revised their *Revised Standard Version* of the Bible in order to accommodate the feminists and their supporters. One of those aiding in the lectionary project is feminist Virginia Ramey Mollenkott. Both of these non-sexist revisions have done violence to the texts. The Evangelical Lutheran Church in America issued a handbook for speakers, writers and editors, *Guidelines for Inclusive Use of the English Language*. While these guidelines may help church workers to tread gingerly on the slippery slopes of inclusivism and politically correct thought, they defy biblical texts and correct doctrine.

Many feminists believe that patriarchal males authored the Bible; therefore, the Bible is a "male-centered book." Feminists insist that nearly everything in it is biased, distorted, or contrived to suppress women; consequently, Scriptures must be "depatriarchalized."[9] Feminist theologian Elisabeth Florenza states, "In theological terms, they (biblical texts) must be exposed as the words of men. Otherwise, Christian discourses about God continue ultimately to legitimize patriarchal oppression."[10]

Other feminists have concluded that "distortions" contained in the Bible are so far removed from truth that biblical texts must be "re-imagined" from the perspective of the women within the accounts. Thus, feminists retell or rewrite the stories of the Bible, not according to existing texts but as they imagine the women involved would have

155

related the events. This concept represents the basis of the RE-Imagining Conference sponsored by the WCC.

One example of re-imagining cited by Elisabeth Florenza concerned the account of John the Baptist's execution as told by Herodias, wife of King Herod. According to this re-imagined account, Herodias insists that Mark distorted the truth about her. She desires to set the record straight, once and for all, because she feels "exploited" by Mark's account. "We, women, are always outside — entering only to delight men or take the blame," she exclaims. Herodias concludes:

> My Sisters, I reach across the centuries to speak to you today: In your search for truth about women of the past — even women of biblical times — beware — because often what you find are stories by men about women.[11]

Re-imagining by the feminists has brought other bizarre and conflicting conjectures about how things really were in Bible times. For example, at the RE-Imagining Conference sponsored by the WCC, one feminist theologian suggested that Mary and Martha were not sisters in the physical sense, but lesbians, making them "foresisters" to all lesbians. Florenza quotes from R. Conrad Wahlberg's book *Jesus According to a Woman,* which postulates another possibility for the difficulties between Mary and Martha:

> Could there indeed have been sexual jealousy between the sisters for the attention of Jesus? Or was it platonic, a friendly relationship? As lively, physical human beings we cannot discount the possibility that there was more than friendly interaction between the three (Jesus, Mary and Martha), a factor which could have entered into the resentment Martha expresses.[12]

Some feminist theologians argue that certain women mentioned in the New Testament were apostles and evangelists, but males suppressed that fact when they wrote the Scriptures. Mary Magdalene was actually an apostle, according to one feminist. Other feminists claim that parts of the Bible were written by women, such as the Gospels of Mark and John, as well as parts of Luke. Nearly 100 years ago, Adolf von Harnack proposed that Prisca authored the book of Hebrews.[13]

According to feminist theologians, the authors of the New Testament were actually the revisionists, endeavoring to hide the fact that Jesus had opened Christian ministry to women, treating them as equals with men in terms of church authority. Feminist theologians believe that they have recovered the original message and mission of Jesus — the liberation and full equality of women. Elisabeth Florenza states:

Readers of the Bible are generally not aware that biblical histories are neither reports of events nor transcripts of facts but rather rhetorical constructions that have shaped information available to them in light of their religious or political interests.[14]

THE WORLD COUNCIL OF CHURCHES' RE-IMAGINING CONFERENCE

The World Council of Churches' RE-Imagining Conference, held in Minneapolis, Minnesota, November 1993, needs more than a little imagination to comprehend. More than 2000 women from 27 countries and all 50 states attended. Most mainline churches were well represented. Reportedly 390 United Methodists were in attendance, including denominational staff and employees. The Evangelical Lutheran Church in America's representation exceeded 300 persons, including about 20 staff members from Chicago headquarters. A news reporter who covered the conference stated:

They're not just talking about new language that's gender-neutral or new images for experiencing Christianity. They've gone beyond that to find new ways to experience human understanding of the divine. They are exploring the sensual and sexual side of the divine, rooting around in contemplative and introspective interplay with God and talking about women's daily experiences of the divine in every culture as central to theology today. They are reshaping Christian understandings of such elemental issues as suffering, and lifting up the voices of ordinary people as foundations of theology.[15]

One of the most outrageous activities undertaken at the RE-Imagining Conference centered around the feminine goddess Sophia. Goddess worship is being systematically promoted within mainline churches by radical feminists and their supporters. "We don't want people to think this is some goddess worship we've cooked up," said Sue Seid-

Martin, instructor in ritual studies at the School of Divinity at the University of St. Thomas in St. Paul, Minnesota. "Sophia is the suppressed part of the biblical tradition, and clearly the female face of the human psyche."[16]

One prayer offered to the goddess Sophia at the conference stated:

> Our sweet Sophia, we are women in your image: With nectar between our thighs we invite a lover, we birth a child; with our warm body fluids we remind the world of its pleasures and sensations ... We celebrate the fingertips vibrating upon the skin of a love ... We celebrate the tongue which licks the wound or wets our lips ... Our guide, Sophia, we are women in your image: With our moist mouths we kiss away a tear, we smile encouragement. With the honey of wisdom in our mouths, we prophesy a full humanity to all the peoples.[17]

This disgusting prayer to the goddess Sophia in which visions of sexual secretions were conjured up, should have spawned a holy rebellion from at least a few of the many mainline church leaders present. Not even a whimper of protest was offered. Christians whose church bodies are affiliated with the World Council of Churches should demand that church officials dissociate the denomination from the WCC's apostasies.

Steve Beard, editor of *Good News,* a magazine for evangelicals in the United Methodist Church, described other activities at the RE-Imagining Conference.

> At one point in the conference, Melanie Morrison, co-founder of Christian Lesbians Out Together (CLOUT), requested time to celebrate "the miracle of being lesbian, out and Christian." Then she invited all other lesbian, bisexual, and transsexual women to join hands and encircle the stage. Religious News Service estimates that "roughly 100 women converged upon the dais, many smiling ... Many of the women remaining in the audience rose to their feet and began to applaud."

> In a workshop called "Prophetic Voices of Lesbians in the Church," Nadean Bishop, the first "out" lesbian minister called to an American Baptist church, claimed that Mary and Martha in the Bible were lesbian "foresisters". She said they were not sisters, but lesbian lovers.

Janie Spahr, a self-avowed lesbian clergywoman in the Presbyterian Church U.S.A. who was prevented by that denomination from serving a local church, claimed that her theology is first of all informed by "making love with Coni," her lesbian partner. She then gave this challenge: "Sexuality and spirituality have come together — and Church, we're going to teach you!"

Judy Westerdorf, a United Methodist clergywoman from Minnesota, told the workshop that the Church "has always been blessed by gays and lesbians ... witches, ... shamans." She joked about the term "practicing homosexual," noting that her partner says she's not practicing, she's pretty good.

The "RE-Imagining" event presented a smorgasbord of cultural ideas and religions, allowing attendees to pick and choose. "Be speculative," participants were told by conference organizers, "there is no 'answer.' We can't imagine what God is like. Being together in our own images is the ultimate."

Many doctrines essential to orthodox Christianity were repudiated at this conference, often in a spirit of derision. This includes the doctrine of God, the deity of Christ, his atoning death, the sinfulness of humanity, creation, the authority of Scriptures, the church, and the biblical understanding of human sexuality.

Regarding the passage from Joel ("I shall pour out my spirit on all humanity"), Lois Wilson, immediate past president of the World Council of Churches, asked, "Surely God didn't mean all humanity; did he mean neo-pagans, did she mean the Wiccans, the Sikhs, the Muslims, the Hindus, the men and women? Or did she?"

Another presenter, Asian feminist theologian Kwok Pui-Lan, indicated that the humanistic-Confucian tradition emphasizes the propensities in human nature for good, not evil. Barbara Lundblad, a Lutheran pastor, (Evangelical Lutheran Church in America) acknowledged: "Some would call our worship of last night verging on heresy ... We did not last night name the name of Jesus. Nor have we done anything in the name of the Father, and of the Son, and of the Holy Spirit." Laughter and cheers followed her observation.

159

Presenter Delores S. Williams, a "womanist" theology professor at Union Theological Seminary in New York City, said, "I don't think we need a theory of atonement at all." Her remark was greeted by applause. "Atonement has to do so much with death," she said. "I don't think we need folks hanging on crosses and blood dripping and weird stuff." Continuing, she said: "We do not need atonement, we just need to listen to the god within ... If Jesus conquered sin, it was in the wilderness and life, not his death (resurrection). The first incarnation of God was not 'some dove on the shoulder,' but in Mary and her body."[18]

Virginia Ramey Mollenkott, an avowed lesbian and former head of the National Council of Churches, told the assembly at the RE-Imagining Conference, "We're taking things forward in a way Luther and Calvin couldn't imagine." She further stated:

"Sin" would be described as wrong relationship, as a collective system of coercion that is leading humankind toward self-destruction. "Salvation" would mean turning away from the constricted attitudes of the world's fear-driven consensus — fear and guilt-driven consensus.

An important part of that would be showing honor to every world religion not just to Christianity. So, "missionary efforts" would target only those people who seem to have no sense of the holy, no experience of an incandescent wonder. There would be dialogue and interaction with people from different religious traditions and there would be mutual modification of the kind that Dr. Chung was discussing, but there would be no more imperialistic atttempts to "make others such as I".[19]

Church bodies represented at the RE-Imagining Conference included the American Baptist Church, the United Church of Christ, the Presbyterian Church U.S.A., the United Methodist Church, the Evangelical Lutheran Church in America, and the Church of the Brethren. Church officials heard from outraged members who had read press reports of the conference that promoted pagan worship, lesbianism and general attacks on fundamental Christian doctrines. Members of the Presbyterian Church U.S.A. were rightly upset when they learned that the largest amount of financial support for the conference was $66,000, given from the Bi-centennial Fund of their denomination. Steve Beard also listed the ELCA and the American Baptist Church as funding sources.[20]

United Methodist Bishop Earl G. Hunt of Lake Junaluska, North Carolina, had strong words of opposition regarding the RE-Imagining Conference. According to George W. Cornell of the Associated Press, Hunt said, "... deifying Sophia is an attempt to reconstitute the godhead ... No comparable heresy has appeared in the church in the last 15 centuries."[21] In fact, the RE-Imagining Conference went far beyond heresy and into apostasy.

Not all comments by church leaders were negative, however. Several defended their denomination's participation around the altars of Sophia. Bishop Herbert Chilstrom, in a letter to synodical bishops of the ELCA, dated February 2, 1994, lauded Barbara Lundblad's presentation at the Re-Imagining Conference, "I believe the conference would have been poorer without Barbara Lundblad's assertion in her presentation that, amidst the prejudice against women that she has experienced in the church, what keeps her in the church is the call of Jesus."

The RE-Imagining Conference, sponsored by the WCC and supported by so many people from mainline denominations, may well have succeeded in blaspheming the Holy Ghost. This conference was not an aberration; it was a portrayal of the spiritual bankruptcy afflicting the WCC and many of its member church bodies. This RE-Imagining Conference is part of a movement which includes the Parliament of World Religions, Thanksgiving Square, hundreds of New Age and global organizations — all endeavoring to bring about the establishment of a one-world, paganistic religion.

FEMINISTS AND THE GODDESS MOVEMENT

It goes by many names — women's spirituality, feminist spirituality, or the goddess tradition. The Bible calls it idolatry. The goddess tradition which springs from feminist attempts to redefine deity has a close alliance with witchcraft and the New Age movement. The goddess tradition is practiced in mainline Protestant churches, in the Roman Catholic Church, within secular feminist circles and, of course, by New Age groups. Its growth is phenomenal. Shelves in religious and secular bookstores are lined with goddess books. Even goddess coloring books have been created to train children in the goddess tradition.

Lois Blinkhorn of the *Milwaukee Journal* interviewed a Dominican nun who has "moved slowly toward a new understanding of spirituality, searching for a bridge between the patriarchal Christian tradition and an earlier female-centered world." The Dominican who celebrated her 50th anniversary as a nun stated, "I come out of a Christian base, but for a long time, I've been drawn to develop woman spirituality in the Goddess tradition. I've struggled and struggled with that bridge — I felt a real tension. It was a very unsure path." Now, according to the reporter, the nun "speaks of reclaiming Mary, the mother of Jesus, as a Goddess, rather than a passively sweet figure, of honoring the elements that tie us to the Earth rather than attempting to dominate them." [22]

The same news report described the experiences of a woman named Amanda who directed Christian education in the Methodist Church for 20 years.

> About 10 years ago, she took a two-year spiritual formation course in Nashville, Tenn., sponsored by the United Methodist Church. "I applied, got in and cried for two years," she says. "It was like coming home to my own spirituality." ... For Amanda, spirituality means attention to God's spirit not only within herself, but also in others, then responding to that spirit. She considers this a return to the experiential quality of the early Christian church, before rigid doctrine developed. "Within the church we let our theology define our spirituality," she says.[23]

Wanda Marrs in her book *New Age Lies To Women* examined the teachings of feminist Rosemary Ruether. Ruether maintains that women became exploited when the Christian male God became dominant. Ruether said, "Suddenly all is ended, paradise is lost, a dark age overtakes the world ... the Great Goddess is replaced by a stern and vengeful God." According to Ruether, the only way to restore women to their rightful place is to return to the mother goddess. Ruether stated, "She who was revered and worshiped by early man because of her power to see the unseen will once again be the pivot ... as divine woman." Men will join the ranks of goddess worshippers with great joy, according to Ruether. Men "will feel it their highest happiness to submit with gratitude to the beneficent power of womanly sympathy. In a word, Man will in those days kneel to Woman, and to Woman alone." [24]

Can you imagine a feminist with these views being invited to speak at seminaries of the Evangelical Lutheran Church in America, or of other church bodies?

Feminists, New Agers, and environmentalists join together in worship of Gaia, the Greek earth goddess. An article in a national periodical provided the following description of earth worshipers:

> To mark Earth Day, four women and two men stood on a hilltop outside Mount Horeb, Wisconsin, literally praying to Mother Earth. "Sacred Earth Power, bring healing to Planet Earth," intoned barefoot Selena Fox, priestess of Circle Sanctuary ... Similar nature worship was part of Earth Day festivals from Boston ... to Berkeley ... The ceremonies were part of a growing U.S. spiritual movement: Goddess worship, the effort to create a female-centered focus for spiritual expression.[25]

It is interesting to note that the last book of the New Testament refers to the mother goddess of end-times as the "Whore of Babylon."

THE ORDINATION OF WOMEN

The issue of a woman's right to be ordained does not center on equality, but on woman's position according to the Scripture. God has assigned men and women differing roles and responsibilities within church and society. These roles and responsibilities do not diminish their relationships to Christ or to one another.

Man and woman's chief role in life is to glorify God. Men have been assigned to give spiritual leadership to their wives, their families and the church. Male leadership is a servant role, not one of domination or iron-fisted control (Ephesians 5:22-33), accomplished through obedience to His Word. As well as bearing and raising children, women are to be "helpmeets" to their husbands (Genesis 2:18, Proverbs 31:10-31). These duties do not preclude women from working outside the home, but nothing should be elevated above their marriages or the rearing of children. Men and women are joined in marriage to sustain one another, replenish the earth with children, and enjoy the fulfillment of God's will for their lives together (Genesis 2:24; Proverbs 18:22). Those who remain single may also know the joy of fulfilling God's will as they live in obedience to His Word. All men and women believers are gifted by the Holy Spirit for ministry in the church and home (1 Corinthians 12), but these gifts are not to be employed in ways which conflict with the biblical principle that men are to provide spiritual leadership for the home and the church (1 Timothy 2:11).

Confusion over the roles of men and women in the church and society has brought great destruction upon families. Women and men who endeavor to function without relating to one another, as in homosexual relationships, are living in rebellion to God's divine order. Women who usurp spiritual leadership in the churches are also acting in defiance of God's Word. The church is not a democracy. Truth and the application of biblical principles are not based on majority rule. The fact that church conventions authorize the ordination of women, in direct violation of the Scriptures, does not justify the decision.

Many men have abandoned their God-given roles as spiritual leaders of their homes. In numerous cases, women have had to assume this responsibility in order that their children would be spiritually guided. God bless these women! The same may be said within the churches. In far too many congregations, men have refused to exercise spiritual leadership, requiring women to assume their responsibilities and duties. Again, God bless these women, but these things ought not to be.

Congregations and church bodies that operate under the biblical leadership of men are greatly blessed. However, it must also be said that congregations whose boards (pastors too) are comprised of persons who are not born again or walking in the Spirit of God are the most grievous of all leadership options. Personally, I would rather live under the leadership of godly women than to function under the authority of men who do not have a living relationship with the Lord.

In addition to the witness of the Scriptures regarding roles of men and women, we also have models which God established in both the Old and New Testaments.

The Old Testament Model

God, operating under His own standard of giving spiritual leadership to men, established the priesthood for the tabernacle and the temple (Exodus 28:1). By God's design, the priesthood included men only. There is not one exception to this directive in the Scriptures. Those who say the "men only" priesthood was based on the culture of that age are denying the inspiration of the Bible. Obviously, God did not have to wait until the 20th century to authorize women to serve as priests or pastors, nor did He have to wait for the evolution of women's rights to open the doors of ordained ministry for women.

God established the pattern of the priesthood for men according to the order of His creation. Feminists have discarded the revealed Word of God because they do not agree with its standards. Their goddess churches (called women churches) have new standards which the feminists themselves are writing. And guess who's in charge?

The New Testament Model

When the time came for Jesus to choose His apostles, He selected 12 men (Luke 6:12-16). Was Jesus also a victim of His culture, unable to achieve His true desire to liberate women, as the feminists would have us believe? Did Jesus lack the courage to appoint women to the apostleship? After all, His enemies could not have inflicted greater harm on Him than the cross. Or, did Jesus actually appoint women to be apostles and the Gospels are contrived pieces of deception as the feminists charge? Jesus chose 12 men as apostles in keeping with the divine order of creation. Until the middle of this century, there was little doubt regarding this matter within Christianity.

According to the book of Acts, when the time came to choose a successor for Judas Iscariot, two men were put forward (Acts 12:21-26). Why did the church not choose women on this occasion? Why did the Holy Spirit not reveal then what He has supposedly revealed in our day? Was the Holy Spirit also required to wait for 20th-century enlightenment before He could right this supposed wrong? Those who endorse process theology, taught in nearly all mainline seminaries, believe in the evolution of truth. The Holy Spirit will not reveal anything in any generation that is contrary to the revealed Word of God. The concept of an evolutionary revelation on the part of the Holy Spirit is not only heresy — it is also utter nonsense! God's Word is complete!

When the apostles needed help and sought to appoint elders, the church was instructed to find seven men of good reputation (Acts 6:1-7). Again why were women not chosen for these positions? The same answer applies — God placed the mantle of spiritual leadership upon men in both family and church. One has to deny the divine inspiration of Scriptures to get past this truth.

Throughout the New Testament, instructions are given for the choosing of elders, bishops and pastors. In every case, Scriptures specify men. (1 Timothy 3 and Titus 1). Paul's instruction that women should not teach or have authority over men in the church (1 Timothy 2:11,12) was not a chauvinistic idea, nor was it just his cultural or religious training. The Holy Spirit spoke through Paul regarding the roles of men and women in the home and church.

Church bodies that ordain men only to the office of the ministry are biblically correct, but they are increasingly being pressured by feminists and their supporters to abandon that policy. In the next few years, it is likely that several more church bodies will abandon policies of ordaining men only. The battle over the ordination of women is underway in several denominations, including the Lutheran Church-Missouri Synod. It is a well documented fact that most denominations which now ordain women are moving faster into heresy and apostasy. The laity must realize that if their church body decides to ordain women, their perverted theology and feminist agenda will not be far behind.

WOMEN SERVE THE LORD WITH DISTINCTION

Every Christian congregation owes a tremendous debt to its women. Women have given, and continue to give, loyal service to Christ and His church, both at home and in distant lands. Numerous women have influenced the life of the church through their writings, hymns, books and articles. As teachers, women have helped to mold the characters of youth, inspiring many to full-time Christian service. Christian women have been, and continue to be, generous with their money and spiritual gifts. Often women serve the Lord with God-given creativity through music and the arts or in ways behind the scenes, neither seeking nor desiring recognition.

Women's missionary societies have long lifted up the banner of world missions. They have consistently supplied the needs of many missionaries. The mission fields have been, and continue to be, homes to countless women with a heart to serve God. None of these important acts requires ordination, nor do they conflict with the Bible. Indeed, they complement the Scriptures in every way and enhance the fellowship of the churches throughout the world.

The Scriptures record numerous accounts of women who faithfully served the Lord with personal sacrifice. Their noble lives are worthy of emulation by both men and women. But in every scriptural narrative, these women served according to the principles of God's Word. None were priests, none were apostles or elders, yet God used them in extraordinary ways.

Queen Esther and Deborah used their positions of influence to serve God and save their people. Who can forget the faith of Hannah, the mother of Samuel, and her supreme devotion to God? Phobe, a deaconess, served the Lord with distinction. Some women, like Priscilla, labored with their husbands in challenging mission work. Others, such as Martha and Dorcas, served in humble, yet significant, ways. These and all other godly women have been honored by the church through the ages, and we honor them and their modern Christian sisters too.

WHO IS ON THE LORD'S SIDE?

Who is on the Lord's side? Who will serve the King?
Who will be His helpers, other lives to bring?
Who will leave the world's side? Who will face the foe?
Who is on the Lord's side? Who for Him will go?
By Thy call of mercy, By Thy grace divine,
We are on the Lord's side – Savior, we are Thine!

Not for weight of glory, not for crown and palm,
Enter we the army, raise the warrior-psalm;
But for Love that claimeth lives for whom He died:
He whom Jesus nameth must be on His side.
By Thy Love constraining, By Thy grace divine,
We are on the Lord's side – Savior, we are Thine!

Jesus, Thou has bought us, not with gold or gem,
But with Thine own life-blood, for Thy diadem.
With Thy blessing filling each who comes to Thee,
Thou hast made us willing, Thou hast made us free.
By Thy grand redemption, By Thy grace divine,
We are on the Lord's side – Savior, we are Thine!

Fierce may be the conflict, strong may be the foe,
But the King's own army none can overthrow.
Round His standard ranging, Victory is secure,
For His truth unchanging makes the triumph sure.
Joyfully enlisting, By Thy grace divine,
We are on the Lord's side – Savior, we are thine!

Frances Havergal 1836-1879

Chapter 11

Contending for the Faith — Pathways to Victory

... Increase in us true knowledge of thee and of thy will, and true obedience to thy Word, that by thy grace we may come to everlasting life; through Jesus Christ our Lord. Amen. ... from a liturgical prayer.

For this is the love of God, that we keep his commandments: and his commandments are not grievous. For whatsoever is born of God overcometh the world: and this is the victory that overcometh the world, even our faith (1 John 5:3,4).

God wills that Christians should win the battles of life. He is the God of Victory, not a god of defeat. The Lord never meant for believers to live in despair or on the bottom of a sea of troubles. As Paul proclaimed, "... we are more than conquerors through him that loved us" (Romans 8:37). In Christ, we are always victors, not victims! Everything required for us to overcome the world and safely reach our destination has been provided by the benevolent hand of our heavenly Father.

While every believer is fully supplied, not every believer appropriates the God-given resources necessary for victory. Soldiers of Christ are derelict in their duty when they fail to put on "the whole armor of God," or when they do not carry the spiritual weapons of warfare into battle. The defeats we experience in life are not due to God's failure to provide, but our own failure to claim all that He freely offers.

JESUS KNOWS OUR EVERY WEAKNESS

God did not send an angel or an emissary to open the way of eternal life for us; He came to earth and lived among us in the Person of Jesus Christ. Our incarnate Savior knows what it is to walk beneath life's crushing load. He knows the weakness of our frame, the pains we bear, the sorrows, heartaches and fears. Jesus has marked out the pathway to eternal life and victory. He asks nothing of us that He Himself has not willingly given, nor does He direct us to go any place where He has not already gone. Most importantly the Lord walks with us every step of the way, through the indwelling presence of the Holy Spirit.

We are children of the King! God's faithfulness is new to us every morning down to the smallest detail. There is nothing in the lives of His children that is beyond the concern of our heavenly Father. Jesus Christ wants us to possess life with a capital "L," having poured out His own life's blood to make it possible.

Living a victorious Christian life can be accomplished only through the strength and power of the Holy Spirit and as we walk in the way of the Lord. The fact that so many Christians have decided to blaze new trails of their own choosing has brought the church to its present pitiful condition. Today the majority of church members are devoid of peace and joy because they foolishly believe their way is better than God's way, or because they have chosen to use their own resources instead of those which God supplies. If the church and individual Christians ever hope to experience revival, they must return to the way of the Lord and walk in true obedience to His Word.

THE PATHWAY OF FAITH

A vast difference exists between fate and faith. The dictionary defines fate as "that which unavoidably befalls one; fortune, or lot." The three goddesses of destiny were known to the Greeks as the Moerae, and to the Romans as the Parcae.[1] It is amazing how many Christians have joined the world in reading horoscopes and consulting astrologers to discover what the "fates" have in store for them. Some church members never miss reading the astrological forecasts in the newspapers, yet they rarely open their Bibles to learn what the Creator God has to say about their futures.

The Bible defines faith as "... the substance of things hoped for, the evidence of things not seen" (Hebrews 11:1). The lives of Christians are not ruled by chance or fate. The destinies of believers are written, not in the stars, but in the Book of Life by the one who died and rose again. As believers living by faith, we place everything we are and hope to be in the hands of our Redeemer whose promises are unfailing. The redeemed of the Lord find no value in reading astrological forecasts to discover their destiny. Instead, they turn to the promises of God's Word, such as Romans 8:28: "And we know that all things work together for good to them that love God, to them who are the called according to his purpose." Those who apprehend God's promises have a joy the world neither knows nor can take away.

I once read an inspiring story of a woman who was suffering from cancer. She and her friends prayed that she might be healed. Believing that God could heal her but not yet knowing His will, she exclaimed, "Either way, I win!"

Paul states in Romans 12:3 that faith is a gift of grace that … cometh by hearing and hearing by the Word of God" (Romans 10:17). We are saved through faith (Ephesians 2:8), justified by faith (Romans 5:1), and baptized into faith (Colossians 2:12). We live by faith (Hebrews 10:38), are kept by the power of God through faith (1 Peter 1:5), are shielded by faith (Ephesians 6:16), and we overcome the world by faith (1 John 5:4). Faith is the essence of everything we believe about God through the revelation of His Word. We are commanded to fight the good fight of faith (1 Timothy 6:12), and to keep the faith until our last breath (2 Timothy 4:7).

The antithesis of faith is unbelief. Faith that is not grounded in the God and Father of the Lord Jesus Christ, believing all He has revealed through His Word and walking in all He has commanded, is no faith at all. Unless we are supernaturally born again by grace through faith into a living relationship with Jesus Christ, we do not possess saving faith, regardless of how many times we have been baptized, confirmed, gone forward during an invitation, how many churches we have joined, how many Bible verses we have memorized or how many good deeds we have done.

Church leaders who are promoting universal salvation through other religions or belief systems are not on the road of faith, but on the road that leads to eternal death. It is no small thing to be part of a denomination that teaches false religion and leads people down the path of destruction. Christian parents should think seriously about the destinies of their children if they continue to fellowship in a church body that treats the Word of God with contempt.

Sometimes the way of faith is a lonely path, especially when people we love refuse to walk with us, or when friends forsake us because they do not understand our commitment to Jesus Christ. It takes grace and courage to stay on the narrow path of faith when friends on the great broad way implore you to join them. Youthful Christians are especially vulnerable to the lures and attractions of our sin-satiated society.

Walking the pathway of faith requires that we uphold truth and oppose everything that is false. That means opposition. Christians who are worth their "salt" will inevitably encounter the hostility of the world because of their stand for the Word of God and the testimony of Jesus. Stephen, converted only a short time before his death, felt the cruel stones of the world's hatred. The death of the first Christian martyr was not a defeat for himself or God, nor was it a victory for Satan; it was just the opposite. Christ was not defeated when He hung on the cross. The saints of God were not defeated when they were thrown into the arena with the lions, or when they were burned at the stake. And we are not defeated when we are subjected to the world's hostility and persecution.

J. Oswald Sanders, in his book *Spiritual Maturity,* observed that God "... delivers some *from* trial, He delivers some *in* trial."[2] Those who endure trial or persecution are blessed indeed for the honor of suffering for His Name, just as Jesus said:

> Blessed are ye, when men shall revile you, and persecute you, and shall say all manner of evil against you falsely, for my sake. Rejoice, and be exceeding glad: for great is your reward in heaven: for so persecuted they the prophets which were before you (Matthew 5:11,12).

The three young men who stood before King Nebuchadnezzar, refusing to bow down and worship the golden image, told the King:

> If it be so, our God whom we serve is able to deliver us from the burning fiery furnace, and he will deliver us out of thine hand, O king. But if not, be it known unto thee, O king, that we will not serve thy gods, nor worship the golden image which thou hast set up (Daniel 3:17,18).

With more and more images of idolatry being erected by our idol-loving culture, Christians on the pathway of faith may be forced to choose between a small but life-saving compromise, or a bold and costly stand for truth. God's Word directs us:

Let us hold fast the profession of our faith without wavering; (for he is faithful that promised;) ... Of how much sorer punishment, suppose ye, shall he be thought worthy, who hath trodden under foot the Son of God, and hath counted the blood of the covenant, wherewith he was sanctified, an unholy thing, and hath done despite unto the Spirit of grace? (Hebrews 10:23,29).

THE PATHWAY OF OBEDIENCE

True faith leads to an understanding of God's will and to true obedience to His Word. Jesus learned obedience through the things He suffered (Hebrews 5:8), "... and became obedient unto death, even the death of the cross" (Philippians 2:8). Our Savior said,

If a man love me, he will keep my words: and my Father will love him, and we will come unto him, and make our abode with him. He that loveth me not keepeth not my sayings: and the word which ye hear is not mine, but the Father's which sent me (John 14:23,24).

The Apostle John wrote, "And hereby we do know that we know him, if we keep his commandments. He that saith, I know him, and keepeth not his commandments, is a liar, and the truth is not in him" (1 John 2: 3,4).

The Old Testament illustrates how Israel learned the lessons of obedience the hard way, as they wandered in the desert 40 years because of their disobedience. When they finally settled in the Promised Land, Israel repeatedly forgot the Lord, defied His laws and suffered the consequences. After they rebelled once too often, God's judgment fell with great severity. The City of Jerusalem and its magnificent temple were destroyed, and the people were exiled from the land for 70 years.

There are those who delight in saying, "The Bible says ...," "The Bible says ...," but they fail to do what the Bible says. Compromise and accommodation are all too common within the church. Vast portions of the organized church have compromised the doctrine of biblical inerrancy, knowing if they acknowledge the Bible as the very Word of God, they can no longer justify their departures from its teachings.

Pastors and individual church members watch as their denomination sinks deeper and deeper into doctrinal error, embracing those things which the Bible condemns. They keep drawing a line in the sand saying, "This far and no farther." However, as doctrinal errors and the acceptance of evils are expanded by the denomination, they keep moving their lines. How far can such compromises be carried out without doing violence to the objective truth of God's Word? How long can Bible-believing Christians remain in their apostate denominations? Pastors are not called by God to protect their pensions, but to protect their parishioners. Church members are not called to pledge their loyalty to a pastor, denomination or to a church building, but to the Lord Jesus Christ. The fact that loved ones are buried in the church cemetery, or that grandpa's name is affixed to a stained-glass window in the sanctuary should not slow a believer's departure from the shrines of apostasy. Francis Schaeffer was right:

> I have said that inerrancy is the watershed of the evangelical world. But it is not just a theological debating point. It is the obeying of the Scripture which is the watershed! It is believing and applying it to our lives which demonstrate whether we in fact believe it.[3]

According to information gathered in a poll and published in *US News and World Report,* more than 80 percent of all Americans claim they believe the Bible is the inspired Word of God. The same poll revealed that 48 percent of those questioned believe "there is no one set of values that is right."[4] If 80 percent of all Americans truly believed that the Bible is the inspired Word of God, our nation would be under the dominion of the greatest revival the United States has ever known. Abortion would be outlawed, homosexual activity would be back under the condemnation of the law, gambling establishments would be shut down, prayer would be in the schools and our churches would be leading the vanguard of national reform. The fact that just the opposite of those things is happening offers a picture of Americans' true views of the Bible. The discrepancy between those who say they believe the Bible is the inspired Word of God and those who believe "there is no one set of values that is right," presents a more accurate assessment of secularized Christianity.

The pathway of obedience is a joyous experience. Those who walk in the ways of the Lord find delight in the results — churches are fruitful, life is sweeter, homes are happier, marriages are stronger, and hearts are at peace. I have never met a person who expressed regret for having walked in the way of obedience to the Word of God, but I have seen an endless parade of broken lives and broken hearts that have chosen the path of human wisdom. The psalmist said it best:

O how I love thy law! it is my meditation all the day. Thou through thy commandments hast made me wiser than mine enemies: for they are ever with me. I have more understanding than all my teachers: for thy testimonies are my meditation. I understand more than the ancients, because I keep thy precepts. I have refrained my feet from every evil way, that I might keep thy word. I have not departed from thy judgments: for thou hast taught me. How sweet are thy words unto my taste! yea, sweeter than honey to my mouth! Through thy precepts I get understanding: therefore I hate every false way (Psalm 119: 97-104).

THE PATHWAY OF SEPARATION

Polycarp, one of the early church fathers and a disciple of John the Apostle, told a story about the beloved apostle when he was living in Ephesus. The story was reported by Irenaeus and, a century later, by Eusebius. According to these early accounts, a false teacher by the name of Cerinthus, who also lived in Ephesus, was teaching many false doctrines, including that Jesus was not born of a virgin but was conceived by natural means. The Apostle John who wanted nothing to do with Cerinthus went out of his way to avoid him.

There are also those who heard from him that John, the disciple of the Lord, going to bathe at Ephesus, and perceiving Cerinthus within, rushed out of the bath-house without bathing, exclaiming, "Let us fly, lest even the bath-house fall down, because Cerinthus, the enemy of the truth, is within." [5]

In these days of accommodation and toleration, the pathway of separation is not a crowded thoroughfare. The growing ecumenical movement which promotes religious cooperation, regardless of creed, is sweeping the mainline churches like a giant tidal wave, even to the promotion of fellowship with non-Christian religions. Evangelicals are

175

also cooperating with those whose doctrines and deeds are undeniably unbiblical. Some church leaders and congregations practice what might be called "limited separation." While they would never think of uniting with organizations such as the World Council of Churches, they freely enter into cooperative activities at other levels with those who deny fundamental doctrines.

Today an ever increasing number of Christians seem enamored with the dazzling sights and sounds of the world. In many church circles it is difficult to discern any appreciable difference in personal values from those one might find in secular settings. Holiness of life and conversation are given scant emphasis among vast numbers of those who claim to be Christians, even though the entire New Testament appeals to believers not to become entangled with the world or live by its standards.

The doctrine of separation does not teach that Christians should avoid people of the world in the course of daily life, business or politics; it refers to spiritual associations with those who claim to be a part of Christ but whose confessions and deeds demonstrate the contrary (1 Corinthians 5:9-13). Our refusal to participate in activities sponsored by churches or religious organizations espousing false teachings and practices does not mean that we should be unkind or unloving to members of those groups. To the contrary, we should be both salt and light, offering them a positive witness of the life-changing power of the gospel of Christ.

The doctrine of spiritual separation is directly related to church discipline. Because the church failed to discipline those who promoted false teachings in the past, there is now an unprecedented toleration of false teachings. Today church leaders and theologians are permitted to promulgate heresy and apostasy without even a threat of discipline. Fifty years ago, mainline church leaders permitted false teachers access to their colleges and seminaries. The ranks of false teachers increased until they gained control of the institutions, which eventually led to a complete take-over of congregations and denominational headquarters by the liberals. What could have been easily halted only a few decades ago, through the application of church discipline and the doctrine of separation, is virtually unstoppable today. False doctrines and unbiblical practices have spread like a deadly cancer throughout the church.

THE WAY OF SEPARATION PRODUCES AUTHENTIC CHRISTIANITY

Paul clearly taught that the true Church of Jesus Christ is one: "There is one body, and one Spirit, even as ye are called in one hope of your calling; One Lord, one faith, one baptism, One God and Father of all, who is above all, and through all, and in you all" (Ephesians 4: 4-6). There are true believers in liberal churches and sects. These Christians are part of the one, true Church because they are justified by faith through the Lord Jesus Christ. However, their association with church bodies or sects which falsify the Word of God should be discontinued the moment they come to realize the truth.

There is no basis of fellowship between Bible-believing Christians and church bodies or organizations that openly teach and practice what is contrary to the revealed Word of God. It is not just bad policy for Bible-believing congregations to be part of apostate organizations such as the World Council of Churches or the National Council of Churches, it is a violation of the Word of God. It is not simply inappropriate for Bible-believing Christians to spiritually fellowship with those who teach what is contrary to the Word of God, it is both sinful and spiritually dangerous.

There is no biblical justification for Christians to participate in activities such as the Parliament of World Religions, the RE-Imagining Conference, or to draft covenants of cooperation with those whose doctrines openly violate the teachings of the Bible. The claim that these syncretistic events give opportunity to witness the gospel is made in defiance of the clear teachings of the Word of God which condemns such associations.

The doctrine of separation is a teaching which goes back to the Old Testament times. A primary reference to the doctrine is given by Paul in his letter to the Church in Corinth:

Be ye not unequally yoked together with unbelievers: for what fellowship hath righteousness with unrighteousness? and what communion hath light with darkness? And what concord hath Christ with Belial? or what part hath he that believeth with an infidel? And what agreement hath the temple of God with idols? for ye are the temple of the living God; as God hath said, I will dwell in them and walk in them; and I will be their God, and they shall be my people. Wherefore come out from among them, and be ye separate, saith the Lord, and touch not the unclean thing; and I will receive you, And will be a Father unto you, and ye shall be my sons and daughters, saith the Lord Almighty (2 Corinthians 6:14-18).

In the above passage, Paul refers to teachings of separation presented in Leviticus, Isaiah, Ezekiel and 2 Samuel. Paul affirmed the importance of this doctrine to the churches in Rome, Galatia, Ephesus, Philippi, Colossae and Thessalonica.

The Lord Himself stressed the importance of separation from false teachers and unbiblical practices when He addressed the churches in the Book of Revelation. Jesus Christ commended the church in Ephesus for testing false teachers and rejecting their message. He chastised the churches in Pergamum and Thyatira for their toleration and promotion of false doctrines.

The Greek word Paul used to describe "separation" in 2 Corinthians 6, is found in nine other New Testament passages. It is always used to describe the absolute separation of God's people from the wicked and unclean. Only a separated people walking in righteousness will be accepted by God. Our righteousness is imputed, of course, as Paul made clear when he referred to the passage in 2 Samuel, "I will be his father, and he shall be my son." Holiness is not attained through our own merits, but through the finished work of Christ and the sanctifying grace of the Holy Spirit. We walk on the pathway of separation, not in order to become a righteous people, but because we are a righteous people.

Every true believer, as well as every Bible-believing church, should be walking the pathway of separation — set apart for God and separated from all that stands in opposition to His revealed truth. We may be ridiculed and misunderstood. We may be labeled as intolerant or unloving, but our joy is to walk with the Lord who leads us in the "paths of righteousness for his name's sake."

THE PATHWAY OF PRAYER

The pathways of victory which we are considering are all one. Each blessing and experience along the way leads to the next, and all are bound together. Though all the pathways have special meaning, it would be difficult to surpass the joy experienced by those who walk the pathway of prayer. Like Mary Magdalene at the garden tomb, we are overwhelmed to be in the presence of the risen Savior. On this pathway we commune as friend with friend, casting all our cares on Him because He cares for us (1 Peter 5:7). In seasons of distress, words are often inadequate and unnecessary as the Spirit makes"... intercessions for us with groanings which cannot be uttered" (Romans 8:26).

Jesus is our supreme example in prayer. The Bible records times when Christ was engaged in prayer all night long. His prayer-life became so attractive to his disciples that they finally implored him, "Lord, teach us to pray." If Jesus needed prayer in His life, how much more do we need prayer as we journey through life? The battle to win our salvation may have been fought at Calvary, the shouts of triumph may have reverberated on Resurrection morning, but surely the victory was won through the prayers which Christ offered in the Garden of Gethsemane where He yielded to the will of His Father and drained the cup of our redemption.

Those who contend for the faith must be undergirded in prayer. God is ready to supply every need for faithful soldiers of the cross. Prayer is the power that sends Satan and his legions fleeing. Prayer is vital to thwart the plans of the enemy and advance the Kingdom of God, and prayer keeps the believer from becoming discouraged or alarmed over the strength of the opposing forces. The Bible directs believers to put on the whole armor of God before engaging the enemy. Paul mentions five pieces of armor which every soldier must wear, and five times he reminds us to pray (Ephesians 6). If Christians truly understood the power of prayer to alter circumstances, or the activity produced in heaven when believers pray, we would scarcely desire to get off our knees.

After returning from a missionary endeavor, the disciples reported to Jesus about their inability to cast out a demon from a possessed man, and asked Him why their efforts had been unsuccessful. Jesus first spoke about their unbelief, then He told them, "Howbeit this kind goeth not out but by prayer and fasting" (Matthew 17:21). Andrew Murray once said:

> Prayer is the one hand with which we grasp the invisible. Fasting is the other hand, the one with which we let go of the visible. ... Fasting helps to express, to deepen, and to confirm the resolution that we are ready to sacrifice anything, even ourselves, to attain the Kingdom of God.[6]

179

When we look upon our sinful nation tottering on the brink of disaster, or when we consider the church's desperate need for revival, we recognize that earnest prayer is required to turn things around. Few Christians understand the power contained in combining prayer and fasting, but it is time to learn. Prayer and fasting need to become a regular part of every Christian's strategy to attack the strongholds of the enemy.

Congregations should have appointed times for members to gather and pray for one another's needs, for the needs of the whole Body of Christ, and for the problems which challenge our nation. Prayer unites our hearts with the will of God and helps us to apprehend the truth that the battle is the Lord's, not ours. God never intended for us to devise the plans, then ask Him to bless what we have determined to do. If committees and church boards spent more time in prayer and less time doing business, more of God's work would be accomplished. The ritual of offering a brief prayer before meetings and activities in order to get on with the "really important things" is a strategy for failure. We are God's servants, called to carry out what He would have accomplished. When congregations turned off the lights on their prayer meetings, they turned off the power to function effectively for the Kingdom of God. When we are too busy to pray, we are too busy. The church needs the vision of prayer expressed by Andrew Murray:

> Who can say what power a church could develop and exercise if it would assume the work of praying day and night for the coming of the Kingdom, for God's power, or for the salvation of souls? Most churches think their members gather simply to take care of and edify each other. They don't know that God rules the world by the prayers of His saints, that prayer is the power by which Satan is conquered.[7]

The Body of Christ has both the assurance of divine guidance and answered prayer when we assemble in the unity and power of the Holy Spirit.

> Again I say unto you, That if two of you shall agree on earth as touching any thing that they shall ask, it shall be done for them of my Father which is in heaven. For where two or three are gathered together in my name, there am I in the midst of them (Matthew 18:19,20).

THE PATHWAY OF WORSHIP

Brief glimpses of worship around the throne of God are presented in the Book of Revelation, but human vocabulary is inadequate to describe the glory. The day Christ died, the veil of the Holy of Holies was rent asunder, signifying that those who are sprinkled by the blood of Christ may approach the throne of God without fear or need of an earthly intermediary. This truth, described in Hebrews 9 and 10, interposes a thrilling invitation:

> Having therefore, brethren, boldness to enter into the holiest by the blood of Jesus, By a new and living way, which he hath consecrated for us, through the veil, that is to say, his flesh; And having an high priest over the house of God; Let us draw near with a true heart in full assurance of faith, having our hearts sprinkled from an evil conscience, and our bodies washed with pure water (Hebrews 10:19-22).

Worship is reserved for God alone (Exodus 20:3; Deuteronomy 5:7; Matthew 4:10). God will not share His glory! The mere suggestion that Christians should be drawn into interfaith activities where other gods are acknowledged is a mockery of the thrice holy God. When reading the Old Testament I have often wondered how the people of Israel dared to worship at the altars of pagan gods when the Lord's hand had been so visible in their midst. What is even more incomprehensible is how those who call themselves Christians can indulge in idolatrous worship at the pagan altars erected by the Parliament of World Religions, by the World Council of Churches or by other interfaith gatherings. If the people of the Old Testament were judged for their idolatrous acts, what judgment must await those who besmirch the blood of Christ and blaspheme His Holy Spirit?

JESUS, NAME ABOVE ALL NAMES

On the pathway of worship the Lord knows us by name — names that He has written in the Lamb's Book of Life. But an even greater wonder awaits us, because He has promised to write His new Name upon us (Revelation 3:12). What an intimate time of celebration! Even now, we may worship the Lord in the beauty of His holiness and praise Him by names already revealed.

181

Believers have found courage and comfort by simply whispering the Name of Jesus during the long watches of the night when their hearts were gripped with fear and doubt. In the Name of Jesus the blind were made to see and the dumb to speak. Peter met a lame man at the temple and commanded him to "rise and walk in the Name of Jesus of Nazareth." The lame man did more than walk; he jumped, leaped and praised the Lord in the sight of all. A short while later, Peter and John were summoned by Jewish leaders and asked by what name or power they had healed the lame man. Peter, filled with the Holy Spirit, responded:

> If we this day be examined of the good deed done to the impotent man, by what means he is made whole; Be it known unto you all, and to all the people of Israel, that by the name of Jesus Christ of Nazareth, whom ye crucified, whom God raised from the dead, even by him doth this man stand here before you whole (Acts 4:9,10).

One day Christ shall appear wearing robes that bear the Name — King of Kings and Lord of Lords. Every knee shall bow and every tongue will confess that Jesus Christ is Lord. Even those who rejected Him will speak His Name in total submission. But on that wonderful day, the redeemed of God shall have already confessed Him as Savior and Lord — We were saved through His Name, baptized in His Name, healed in His Name, commissioned for service in His Name, married in His Name and buried in His Name. Furthermore, we prayed in His Name and worshiped in His Name. There is coming a day when the whole world will comprehend why taking God's Name in vain was no small offense, and why God has exalted above all things His Name and His Word (Psalm 138:2).

NAMES OF GOD IN THE OLD TESTAMENT

The Old and New Testaments record many names which reveal the awesome attributes of the Triune God. Some of these precious names are not often used today because of the difficulty in translating the original Hebrew into English, but we are richer for probing the depths of the divine record.

EL SHADDAI — "God of the Mountain"

"As the mountains are round about Jerusalem, so the Lord is round about his people from henceforth even for ever" (Psalm 125:2). Our lives are secure beneath the towering mountains of El Shaddai's protecting love. The storms of life may rage, the enemy may plot to destroy us, but El Shaddai promises that nothing shall ever separate us from His love. Old Testament references to El Shaddai include Genesis 17:1 and Exodus 6:3.

EL 'ELYON — "God Almighty"

This name, recorded in Genesis 14:18, Numbers 24:16, and several Psalms, reveals God as supreme. No other gods stand before Him. In this world of unpredictable variation, it is comforting to know that El Elyon never changes, nor can His will be subverted by the fleeting powers of earth. The Almighty God who reigns in eternal majesty is our heavenly Father.

JEHOVAH-JIREH — "God Will Provide"

Abraham met Jehovah-Jireh on Mount Moriah where in faith and obedience he offered his only son Isaac to the Lord in certain confidence that God would raise Isaac from the dead (Hebrews 11:19). When Isaac inquired concerning the lamb for their sacrifice, Abraham replied, "My son, God will provide himself a lamb for a burnt offering ..." (Genesis 22:8). Centuries later, God did provide the Lamb in the Person of Jesus Christ. Everything we need in this life or the next is provided by Jehovah-Jireh.

JEHOVAH-SHALOM — "God is our Peace"

The Lord is the God of all peace (Judges 6). The peace which God gives is not based on outward circumstances but on His unbreakable promises. Jehovah-Shalom's peace passes all understanding and a great deal of misunderstanding. Only Jehovah-Shalom, who is also called the Prince of Peace, can solve the problems of our troubled world: "Peace I leave with you, my peace I give unto you: not as the world giveth, give I unto you. Let not your heart be troubled, neither let it be afraid" (John 14:27).

JEHOVAH-SHAMMAH — "God is There"

Jehovah-Shammah is revealed in Ezekiel 48:35. In Isaiah 43:1 and 2, it is written:

... Fear not: for I have redeemed thee, I have called thee by thy name; thou art mine. When thou passest through the waters, I will be with thee; and through the rivers, they shall not overflow thee: when thou walkest through the fire, thou shalt not be burned; neither shall the flame kindle upon thee.

Jesus revealed Jehovah-Shammah when He promised to be with us always, and never leave or forsake us. Jehovah-Shammah is also experienced through the indwelling of the Holy Spirit in all believers.

JEHOVAH-TSIDKENU — "God our Righteousness"

Jeremiah 23 reminds us of God's righteousness, given to those who were once lost and condemned creatures. We have no righteousness except that which comes through Jesus Christ. Jehovah-Tsidkenu revealed Himself in the atoning work of Jesus Christ on Calvary:

Who is the image of the invisible God, the firstborn of every creature ... And he is the head of the body, the church: who is the beginning, the first born from the dead; that in all things he might have the preeminence. For it pleased the Father that in him should all the fulness dwell; And, having made peace through the blood of his cross, by him to reconcile all things unto himself; by him, I say, whether they be things in earth, or things in heaven (Colossians 1:15,18-20).

THE ROCK

The Rock, a name applied to our Lord in Deuteronomy 32, Psalms, Isaiah, and 1 Corinthians, holds a precious truth — Jesus is our "mighty fortress," the solid, immovable rock upon which we stand and upon which our lives rest secure. An understanding of this name helps us to realize why Moses was severely punished when he struck the rock in the wilderness in order to bring forth water, instead of speaking to it as commanded by God. The rock was a type of Christ. The first time the people cried for water, God told Moses to strike the rock, but the second time, he was instructed only to speak to the rock. However, in anger Moses struck the rock, for which he was forbidden to enter the Promised Land. Christ who gives the living water was struck once and for all upon the cross to make full atonement for our sins. Paul explains this to the church in Corinth:

Moreover, brethren, I would not that ye should be ignorant, how our fathers were under the cloud, ... And did all drink the same spiritual drink: for they drank of that spiritual Rock that followed them: and that Rock was Christ (1 Corinthians 10:1,4).

Walking on the pathway of worship, we experience an intimacy with the Lord that is unfathomable and full of glory. His name should always be on our lips, but only in a most reverential manner as Martin Luther declared in the Small Catechism: "We should fear and love God and not curse, swear, conjure, lie or deceive by His name; but call upon His name in everytime of need, and worship Him with prayer, praise and thanksgiving." [8]

THE PATHWAY OF SERVICE

Christians whose spiritual activities are confined to attending church, Bible studies and interest groups may fit the often quoted definition of being "so heavenly minded, they're no earthly good." It is not enough to merely talk about witnessing the gospel, or sharing Christ's love, or standing against the forces of evil. Faith must be put into practice. We are to be "... doers of the word, and not hearers only ..." (James 1:22). Those who contend for the faith cheerfully walk on the pathway of service.

The waters of the Sea of Galilee serve the whole Nation of Israel by providing water for drinking and irrigation. The Jordan River begins in the foothills of Mount Hermon, flows into the northern part of the Sea of Galilee and out its southern side, then it continues southward to the Dead Sea. While the Dead Sea receives the waters of the Jordan, it has no outlet. Consequently, it is the saltiest body of water in the world and devoid of life. Christians whose lives are all take and no give soon resemble the Dead Sea. God intends for us to be like the life-giving Sea of Galilee; He blesses His people that they might be a blessing to others.

Until the beginning of the present century, churches largely provided for the nation's poor and hurting. Colleges, schools, hospitals, orphanages and homes for the aged were all part of the church's benevolent outreach. While many of these works are still carried out by the church, most have been assumed by government. The nation and the church are both poorer for this new arrangement.

Much of the modern church resembles the Church of Laodicea which considered itself as "rich and in need of nothing." While huge sums are being spent by congregations and denominations on extravagant buildings and self-indulging programs, missionary work is put on hold and the desperate needs of multitudes continue unmet. If missions and outreach were given top priority by the churches, our nation and the world could be reached for Christ.

The Great Commission of Christ has not been rescinded. Every Christian is called by the Lord to witness the gospel to those around them. The early church proclaimed the good news of Christ until at last there were saints in Caesar's household (Philippians 4:22). The Lord has instructed His church to pray for more workers to gather in the harvest: "... The harvest truly is great, but the labourers are few: pray ye therefore the Lord of the harvest, that he would send forth labourers into his harvest" (Luke 10:2). Every Christian should have a "hands-on" attitude about spreading the gospel. We are called to witness the good news of Christ where we are, and send others where we ourselves cannot go. Those who are sent should have the financial support and prayers of the church. Every congregation should have a heart for missions. As someone has wisely stated, "A congregation should be known, not for the number it seats, but for the number it sends."

There is no lack of opportunity to demonstrate the love of Christ in this world which is filled with hurting, hungry and heart-broken people. Jesus related the scene of judgment when the nations of the world will be called to account. He compared it to a shepherd separating the sheep from the goats. Because judgment begins with the House of God, the King spoke first to those on his right (His Church), praising them for their love and compassion.

> Then shall the King say unto them on his right hand, Come, ye blessed of my Father, inherit the kingdom prepared for you from the foundation of the world: For I was hungered, and ye gave me meat: I was thirsty, and ye gave me drink: I was a stranger, and ye took me in: Naked and ye clothed me: I was sick, and ye visited me: I was in prison, and ye came unto me (Matthew 25:34-36).

The assembled Church was amazed at the King's words and inquired as to when they had done all the things enumerated. He replied, "... Inasmuch as ye have done it unto one of the least of these my brethren, ye have done it unto me" (Matthew 25:40). Those on the King's left hand were sent away "to everlasting fire prepared for the devil and his angels," because they had failed in all those things.

The Apostle John sheds light on the above passage, making clear that we are not saved because of our works but through the grace of Jesus Christ. True believers demonstrate the love of Christ because their faith is genuine.

> We know that we have passed from death unto life, because we love the brethren. He that loveth not his brother abideth in death. ... But whoso hath this world's good, and seeth his brother have need, and shutteth up his bowels of compassion from him, how dwelleth the love of God in him? My little children, let us not love in word, neither in tongue; but in deed and in truth (1 John 3:14,17,18).

Paul's commentary on this theme is also poignant:

> For by grace are ye saved through faith; and that not of yourselves: it is the gift of God: Not of works, lest any man should boast. For we are his workmanship, created in Christ Jesus unto good works, which God hath before ordained that we should walk in them (Ephesians 2:8-10).

FRANKIE SAN

Kyuzo Miyaishi, known to his friends as "Frankie San," has spent the last 30 years of his life ministering to inmates in the prison system of South Carolina. A native of Japan, Frankie came to this country in 1961 to study at the Lutheran Theological Southern Seminary in Columbia, South Carolina. After completing his studies, he took up residence inside the compound of the Central Correctional facility in Columbia, declaring that God had given him a "life sentence."

Though ordained, Frankie San is not, nor has he ever been, a prison chaplain. His first assignment in the prison was teaching inmates how to read and write. Frankie laughs as he recalls a young Japanese with broken English teaching American men how to read *Cat in the Hat.*

When prison officials could find no one to administer their new library, Frankie took the job. His library is like an oasis in a barren desert — filled with plants, exotic birds, tropical fish and, of course, books.

Each Christmas, Frankie provides small gifts for each of the prison's inmates. Dressed in a Santa suit and wearing a cross around his neck, Frankie goes from cell to cell distributing gifts, reminding the inmates that God still loves them. Often prisoners in lonely cells would lie on their beds and weep as Frankie read the Scriptures and softly sang the strains of familiar carols. Over the years, Frankie's Christmas project has grown to include inmates at other South Carolina prisons, including those housing women and juveniles.

Prisoners who enter Frankie's library often find more than a book; many find Christ through the loving witness of this Japanese missionary to America. Frankie has a unique ministry to inmates on death row, who may come as close to "the least of the brethren" as it is possible to get. Through the years he has led several death-row inmates to confess Jesus Christ as their Savior and Lord.

After South Carolina's death penalty had been reinstated and the first inmate was scheduled to die, Frankie wrote a letter to the governor, sincerely requesting that he be permitted to take the inmate's place in the electric chair. A deeply moved governor invited Frankie to visit his office in order that he might meet the state employee who made such an offer.

At their request Frankie has walked several inmates to the death chamber and stayed with them through their execution. He has opened his home on the prison compound to family members of inmates being put to death, and he has conducted burial services for several who were executed.

Today Frankie has another job in the prison that no one wanted — he ministers to inmates who have AIDS. Frankie's joy is beyond description, as are his compassion and love. You see, he walks with Jesus on the pathway of service, and every day Frankie becomes just a little more like Him.

But thanks be to God, which giveth us the victory through our Lord Jesus Christ. Therefore, my beloved brethren, be ye steadfast, unmoveable, always abounding in the work of the Lord, forasmuch as ye know that your labour is not in vain in the Lord (1 Corinthians 15:57,58).

THE PATHWAY OF LOVE

The pathway of love is considered last, not because it is least important, but because it is the ultimate of the pathways to victory. On this path we come face to face with the incomprehensible love of God. As much as we try, we cannot fathom so great a love for unworthy creatures as ourselves. "But God commendeth his love toward us, in that, while we were yet sinners, Christ died for us" (Romans 5:8). As someone has said, it was God's love, not the nails, that held Christ to the cross. Halfway through eternity we shall still be asking, "How could He love us so?"

When Jesus met Peter a few days after His resurrection, He asked him three times, "Peter, do you love me?" Three times Peter responded, "Lord, you know that I love you." Each time, the Lord instructed him, "Feed my sheep." Feeding, loving, caring and serving flow from hearts of those who have been redeemed by the Savior.

The most difficult aspect of the Christian life is not receiving the unmerited love of God (agape), but sharing it with others. If we are going to effectively contend for the faith, we must learn to love as Christ loved. We must love homosexuals, feminists, liberals, false teachers, abortionists, pornographers, drug pushers, alcoholics, thieves and murders. Loving them does not for one moment sanction anything they represent or promote, but they have souls that need to be saved. Christ made clear that He came to call sinners to repentance. Our commission is not to judge, but to witness Christ's love to a lost and dying world. The Bible and history are filled with accounts of enemies of the church who were converted, including Saul of Tarsus.

Love is not silent when danger threatens those around us. At first, it may seem unkind or even unloving to sound the alarm of impending danger, but those who are rescued will thank us throughout eternity. Those who now brand us as trouble makers and disturbers of the peace will one day come to realize that love prompted our action.

Those who would effectively contend for the faith must love one another. The absence of love that some Christians have for each other is a scandal to the cross. Numerous congregations are in constant upheaval as members turn on one another over the most trivial matters. The enemy of the Church thrills when he sees brothers and sisters in Christ consuming one another in bitter controversies and contentious

189

disagreements. He laughs as believers stumble over obstacles which fellow Christians have thrown in their path. Most of the issues which divide and consume the energies of the average congregation have little or no relevance to the destinies of men's souls.

There is more love and warmth in many liberal churches today than in Bible-believing fellowships where Christians are substituting orthodoxy for love. There is often more compassion in the town tavern than in some congregations when it comes to caring about people whose lives are broken on the wheels of living. Without love, we are only playing church. When love is absent, so is the vision for a lost and dying world.

The difference between a soldier of the cross who is contending for the faith and a militant idealist who fights only for a cause is the love of God shed abroad in our hearts. Who can ignite the spark of agape love and fan it into flame? The One who walks with us on the pathways to victory!

> Spirit of God, descend upon my heart;
> Wean it from earth, through all its pulses move;
> Stoop to my weakness, mighty as thou art,
> And make me love thee as I ought to love.
>
> I ask no dream, no prophet ecstasies,
> No sudden rending of the veil of clay,
> No angel visitant, no opening skies;
> But take the dimness of my soul away.
>
> Hast thou not bid me love thee, God and King:
> All, all thine own, soul, heart and strength and mind?
> I see thy Cross; there teach my heart to cling;
> O let me seek thee, and O let me find!
>
> Teach me to love thee as thine angels love,
> One holy passion filling all my frame:
> The baptism of the heaven-descended Dove,
> My heart an altar, and thy love the flame.
>
> *George Croly, 1780-1860*

JOY BEYOND COMPARE

Thy Word, O God, declareth
   No man hath seen or heard
The joys our God prepareth
   For them that love their Lord.
Their eyes shall see thy glory,
   Thy face, thy throne, thy might;
With shouts shall they adore thee,
   The true, eternal Light.

With thee, their warfare ended,
   Thy saints, from earth released,
Shall keep, with glories splendid,
   Eternal holy feast.
There shall thy sons and daughters
   The tree of life partake,
Shall drink the living waters,
   And bread with thee shall break.

Thy constant praises sounding
   Before thy great white throne,
They all in joy abounding
   Shall sing the song unknown:
Laud, honor, praise, thanksgiving
   And glory ever be
To Thee, the everlasting
   And blessed Trinity.

Johann Walther, 1496-1570

Chapter 12

Contending for the Faith — Encouragement for Battle-Weary Christians

... the joy of the Lord is your strength (Nehemiah 8:10).

For whatsoever things were written aforetime were written for our learning, that we through patience and comfort of the scriptures might have hope. Now the God of patience and consolation grant you to be likeminded one toward another according to Christ Jesus: That ye may with one mind and one mouth glorify God, even the Father of our Lord Jesus Christ (Romans 15:4-6).

As the battle for truth intensifies in both church and society, many Christians are becoming weary and discouraged in the struggle. News reports of further doctrinal erosions and unbiblical practices within the church flow in an unending stream. Persons we dearly love are caught up in this morass of liberalism. How many more battles must we fight? How much opposition must we bear? What possible good can our small efforts accomplish in the cosmic struggle against immorality and false teachers?

When informed Christians try to enlighten others regarding the infiltration of false teachings into their denominations, so few care to listen. Often church leaders respond with a stern rebuke at the mere suggestion that anything in the church could be wrong. Facts and the clear Bible teachings have little sway with church members who place loyalty to a pastor or a denomination over loyalty to Christ and His Word. Rejection is a cross that is not easy to bear.

Letters to political leaders seem to make little impact on the outcome of legislation to legitimatize sin and evil. There are personal discouragements brought on by sorrow, sickness and hardships. Financial reverses, the loss of a job, a rebellious child — these and so many more issues of life tend to wear us down.

But there is good news today for the battle-worn Christian. We are on the winning side of the battle. God knows and cares, and He will do something about the challenges of life confronting us. We can lean on His everlasting arms, knowing victory will be ours through the strength and power of Christ. The cares of God's children are important to Him.

Satan wants you to be discouraged and dysfunctional, unable to accomplish much for the Kingdom of God. He uses every trick in the book to bring depression and discord into your life, robbing you of your joy. On your own, you are no match for his wiles, but the Lord, through His Word and Holy Spirit, promises that He "will never leave or forsake you."

WE ARE NOT ALONE IN THE BATTLES OF LIFE

After Elijah had challenged the false prophets on Mount Carmel, Queen Jezebel tried to kill him. Elijah, the man of God who had fearlessly faced the foe, felt alone and despondent. Then God spoke to him, not in the wind, earthquake or fire, but in the still small voice. There in the wilderness, Elijah discovered that he was not alone, either from heaven's perspective or on earth where God still had 7000 people in Israel who had not bowed their knees to false gods (1 Kings 19).

I too have felt alone many times in the great struggle for truth. What joy was mine to discover that the Savior had many others, near and far, who were ready to lend a hand and offer a word of encouragement. Several years ago when I revealed that Lutheran Social Service of Minnesota was using pornography in its treatment of troubled children, many church leaders connected with LSS of Minnesota attacked me with vengeance. They published distortions and sought to discredit my ministry. But in the midst of that great battle, Dr. James Dobson wrote a letter, affirming my stand and inviting me to be a guest on his radio broadcast. Letters of encouragement by the thousands came from all parts of the United States and Canada. Many letters were from persons who had gone or were going through similar battles. One of the reasons we have established Abiding Word Ministries is to be an encouragement to those who feel alone in their personal struggles within their churches and communities.

You, dear child of God, are not alone in the battle for truth, nor are you alone in your personal struggles. Your heavenly Father never intended that you should bear the responsibility for the Kingdom's work in your own strength or power. Around and beneath God's children are the everlasting arms, sustaining you every moment of the day. As the song reminds us: "Every day is a victory, when you put it in the hands of the Lord." The Lord extends to us this gracious invitation:

Come unto me, all ye that labour and are heavy laden, and I will give you rest. Take my yoke upon you, and learn of me; for I am meek and lowly in heart: and ye shall find rest unto your souls. For my yoke is easy and my burden is light (Matthew 11:28-30).

ENCOURAGEMENT FROM THE SCRIPTURES

"He speaks and the sound of His voice is so sweet the birds hush their singing." Those words from the precious Easter hymn "In the Garden" can become a reality in our hearts every time we open the Holy Scriptures. The Bible is not a rule book or merely a volume of ancient history; "it is living and active." The Scriptures were given for our encouragement "that we might have hope." Daily we need to flee to the fountain of God's Word and draw strength and encouragement from its living waters. As the Psalmist said: "God is our refuge and strength, a very present help in trouble" (Psalm 46:1).

Richard Wurmbrand, a Lutheran pastor who spent 14 years in a Romanian prison for his faith, has said, "The words 'fear not' appear in the Scriptures 366 times, one for each day of the year, and even one for leap year." The wonderful promises contained in God's Word will do us little good unless they are personally appropriated. A meaningful exercise is to read the Bible until you find a personal promise which will take you through the day. Memorize the promise and meditate on its benefits, then pray the promise as you claim it by faith.

ENCOURAGEMENT THROUGH PRAYER

When I was a young boy, I frequently visited with John P. Lafferty, a retired Baptist pastor in our small community. I still have several books in my library which came from his personal collection. It was well known in our small town, Worthington, Pennsylvania, that I wanted to be a preacher when I grew up. John Lafferty had a profound influence in my life. Sitting together on his front porch swing, he often talked with me about Jesus and encouraged me to faithfully serve the Lord.

Frequently I sang for him, while his wife accompanied me on their old pump organ in the parlor. Without fail, Reverend Lafferty, a man of prayer, asked me to sing "Near to the Heart of God." This song has brought me comfort in many a storm of life, as it did to my aged Baptist friend.

There is a place of quiet rest, near to the heart of God,
A place where sin cannot molest, near to the heart of God.

There is a place of comfort sweet, near to the heart of God,
A place where we our Savior meet, near to the heart of God.

There is a place of full release, near to the heart of God,
A place where all is joy and peace, near to the heart of God.

O Jesus, blest Redeemer, sent from the heart of God,
Hold us who wait before thee, near to the heart of God.

Cleland B. McAfee

Our Lord, who is always "more ready to hear than we to pray, more ready to give than we to receive," meets us in the beautiful Garden of Prayer, where He lifts our burdens and carries our sorrows. Prayer seems so elementary, yet we frequently forget to pray! A small plaque on my desk poses a most profound question, "Have You Prayed About It?" How often we wrestle and agonize over problems before taking them to our heavenly Father. A familiar hymn reminds us, "O what peace we often forfeit, O what needless pain we bear, all because we do not carry everything to God in prayer!"

ENCOURAGEMENT THROUGH THE BODY OF CHRIST

One of God's greatest gifts of grace is placing us within the Body of Christ. We are not saved in isolation or required to "go it alone." The Lord places us within the life-nurturing fellowship of His people so that we might have the hands and hearts of fellow believers for strength and support.

Those who have gone through a time of personal hardship and have felt the love and support from fellow believers know the joy of belonging to the family of God. Dr. F. Eppling Reinartz, former president of the seminary that I attended, once told us that the greatest compliment he had ever heard about a congregation came from an old woman who said, "When you come into this church, you never have to bear another burden alone." That is surely what God intended for His church in every place and time.

Paul wrote to the church in Rome, "Now the God of patience and consolation grant you to be likeminded one toward another according to Christ Jesus: That ye may with one mind and and one mouth glorify God, even the Father of our Lord Jesus Christ" (Romans 15:5,6). Our supreme goal as Christians is to glorify God. We need one another to accomplish that goal, and we need one another for personal strength and effectiveness in the Kingdom's work.

When the fellowship of the church is unified through the agape love of God, there is power, warmth and joy in the Body of Christ that cannot be found anywhere else in the world. Knowing that, Satan tries desperately to destroy unity among Christians. Focusing on our weaknesses, Satan is amazingly successful in causing Christians to turn on one another.

It is a sad commentary when Bible-believing congregations are unable to maintain unity in the fellowship. Satan wants to destroy congregations that proclaim salvation and uphold the truth of God's Word. He uses unkind remarks, misunderstandings and differences of opinion to fracture the fellowship. But we must never give in to his wiles.

The church is composed of redeemed sinners who are still in the process of growing in grace. We often fail God and one another. But when those failings are placed under the blood of Jesus, Satan has no means to turn them against us.

Endeavor to be a source of encouragement to your pastor and to fellow believers. Write a note to someone who is going through a trial. Assist someone who needs a helping hand. Let forgiveness flow whenever you are wronged in any way. Don't demand an apology, just forgive as Christ has forgiven you — no strings, no conditions. Be God's instrument of comfort to those around you. And when your heart is heavy, remember to draw strength and encouragement from the family of God.

ENCOURAGED THROUGH THE CALL OF GOD

Though the Israelites were a stubborn, sinful and rebellious people, God placed his seal upon them and delivered them from Egypt's bondage. They belonged to Him, and He would see them safely to the Promised Land. In order to keep their lives centered on Him and provide for their spiritual welfare, God gave them the tabernacle, endowed with His holy presence. The Lord dwelt (tabernacled) with them throughout their long years of wilderness wanderings.

God provided the instructions for the tabernacle's construction, even to the smallest details of its furnishings. He needed many dedicated hands for such a noble work, as well as men to supervise the construction of the tabernacle and direct the crafting of its appointments. Thus in His infinite wisdom God chose from all the tribes of Israel those extraordinary and outstanding men — Bezalel and Oholiab! (Exodus 31).

The fact that Bezalel and Oholiab are not well known or listed among the great heroes of the Bible does not lessen their standing before God. Heaven will be filled with the obscure, long-forgotten servants of the Most High — forgotten by this world's conceptions of greatness, but long remembered and highly exalted in heaven where greatness is reckoned by God's standards.

Bezalel and Oholiab were not chosen because they were gifted — they were gifted because they were chosen. God told Moses that He had called Bezalel by name and "filled him with the spirit of God, in wisdom, and in understanding, and in knowledge, and in all manner of workmanship," and that He had chosen and gifted Oholiab as well. What an honor it is to be chosen by God, and so we are if we have been redeemed through Jesus Christ. What an incredible thrill when the heavenly Father taps you on the shoulder and calls you to undertake a task for Him.

Everyone the Lord calls, He empowers with all necessary abilities. All our abilities, natural and otherwise, are God-given; each must be sanctified on the altar of single-minded commitment if we are to be of service to the Lord. The wreckage of well-intentioned tasks lie strewn about the church today, the unhappy results of persons trying to do a work for God through their own resources.

A young man who had just completed his first year of seminary training was invited to preach in his home congregation. He was more than a little anxious to prove himself as a student of Scripture and as an effective proclaimer of the Word. He eagerly awaited his moment in the service, and at last it came. As he stepped into the pulpit and beheld a sea of familiar faces — all intently looking at him, all waiting for him to speak — panic seized him. He stood in the pulpit frozen with fear. His message lay hidden from reach. He broke from the pulpit in a flood of embarrassment and tears. His pastor went to him and said, "Son, if you had entered the pulpit in the manner you left it, God could have used you."

The Lord does not need our abilities or successes. He wants us — willing and obedient. When God determined to have the tabernacle erected in the center of the Israelite camp, He did not direct Moses to enlist the services of highly trained artisans, and have a go at it. The tabernacle was to be fashioned after the Tabernacle of God in heaven; it would depict the redemptive story of His Son at Calvary many centuries later. Every part of the tabernacle had to be exact and true. To that end, God called and gifted Bezalel and Oholiab to carry out the tasks He desired to accomplish.

Today the Lord is building His Church, not according to the standards of the world, but upon the foundational truth of His Word. The gates of hell shall not prevail against Her. God's plan to bring salvation to this lost and dying world is not a plan loosely created, or one that can be left to the whims and best devices of men. The Lord of the Church has revealed His plan and His will in His holy and inerrant Word. Through the Holy Spirit, He has gifted and empowered His Church to accomplish His purposes. Christians should carry out their respective assignments in joyful obedience to God's Word. The fact that you feel unqualified, unprepared or even unsuited to assume a specific work for the Lord may be your greatest qualification.

ENCOURAGEMENT THROUGH PRAISE

A marvelous story of encouragement is found in 2 Chronicles 20. King Jehoshaphat was told, "A vast army is coming against you."

Immediately the king with all the men of Judah, with their wives, children and little ones, stood before the Lord. The king prayed, reminding God of His promise:

... O Lord God of our fathers ... (You said) "If, when evil cometh upon us, as the sword, judgment, or pestilence, or famine, we stand before this house, and in thy presence, ... and cry unto thee in our affliction, then thou wilt hear and help" (2 Chronicles 20: 6,9).

The answer of the Lord came quickly:

Ye shall not need to fight in this battle: set yourselves, stand ye still, and see the salvation of the Lord with you, O Judah and Jerusalem: fear not, nor be dismayed; tomorrow go out against them: for the Lord will be with you (2 Chronicles 20:17).

Jehoshaphat appointed singers to go before the army, praising the Lord as they went to meet the invading armies. As they began to sing, "the Lord set ambushments against the children of Ammon, Moab, and mount Seir, which were come against Judah," and the armies turned on one another. When Jehoshaphat and his men arrived, all that was left to do was carry off the spoils! After four days of gathering plunder, Jehoshaphat and his army assembled again to praise the Lord. When they returned to Jerusalem, they assembled at the temple with harps and lutes and trumpets and praised the Lord once more.

Hymns, psalms and praises were never meant to be "fillers" for a worship service or devices of entertainment. There is power in praise. Praise lifts the heart to the throne of God and unleashes a power to overtake the gates of hell. The grand old hymn of the church "Onward Christian Soldiers," that is viewed by some denominations as being too militant, has been dropped from their hymnals. However, the hymn offers many vital truths regarding spiritual warfare, as in the second verse:

At the sign of triumph Satan's legions flee;
On then Christian soldiers, on to victory!

Hell's foundations quiver at the shout of praise;
Brothers lift your voices, loud your anthems raise!

Onward, Christian soldiers, marching as to war,
With the cross of Jesus going on before!

On the front cover of this book is an artist's sketch of a sculpture which graces the front of the Cathedral Church of St. Michael in Coventry, England. During World War II, the Coventry Cathedral was destroyed by Nazi bombs. The Church of St. Michael was constructed adjacent to the preserved ruins of the bombed-out cathedral. Sir Jacob Epstein's sculpture of Archangel Michael standing over Satan who is bound in chains depicts the inevitable triumph of the Church over Satan and all the forces of evil. It is a truth we need to focus upon as the battle rages.

As Christians, we can never lay down our burden of contending for the faith that was once delivered unto the saints until Jesus comes or until He calls us home to glory. We must realize that our personal stand for truth is our God-given duty. As long as souls are lost in sin, we must press on with the only message of hope this world will ever hear. As long as there are those who are determined to attack and undermine the foundations of the faith, we must faithfully stand together. We do not stand in our own strength, but in the mighty power of the Holy Spirit.

May God help us to be faithful as we fight the good fight of faith! The future of our families, our churches and our nation are at stake. We must never yield one inch of blood-bought ground to the enemy of our souls. The archangel Michael will, one day, stand victorious over the conquered enemy. "And the God of peace shall bruise Satan under your feet shortly..." (Romans 16:20). Let us "earnestly contend for the faith which was once delivered unto the saints." As the hymn-writer reminds us, "This day the noise of battle, the next, the victor's song."

Now unto him that is able to keep you from falling,
and to present you faultless
before the presence of his glory
with exceeding joy,

To the only wise God our Saviour,
be glory and majesty,
dominion and power,
both now and ever, Amen.

201

NOTES

CHAPTER 2   Contending – our Duty

1. *American Family Association Journal,* P.O. Box 2440, Tupelo, Ms 38803.
2. Term used by Francis Schaeffer.
3. Rodney G. Lensch, *Rod and Staff Newsletter,* Vol. XVI, No. 64, Winter, 1993.
4. Robert Franklin, "Little Six grants $500,000 to Council of Churches," *Star Tribune,* December 3, 1993, p. 4 B.

CHAPTER 3   Contending – Faith of our Fathers

1. P. Ljostveit, *Intermission Church History,* p.110.
2. Henry C. Sheldon, *History of the Christian Church,* Vol. II, p. 411.
3. John Foxe, *Foxe's Book of English Marytrs,* p. 48.
4. P. Ljostveit, op. cit., p.113.
5. Matthew Spinka, an essay based on his book *John Hus at the Council of Constance,* (New York:Columbia University Press, 1965), published in *Our Voices,* and *Czechoslovak Weekly,* Toronto, Canada.
6. P. Ljostvet, op. cit., p.380.
7. *Morning Glory,* Hauge Lutheran Innermission, 2016 Elton Hills Drive N.W., Rochester, MN 55901.
8. Carl McIntire, *Outside the Gate,* p. 285.
9. Herman J. Otten, *Baal or God,* p. 134.
10. Ibid., p. 221.
11. Edith Schaeffer, *The Tapestry,* p. 189.

CHAPTER 4   Contending – not Denominational Distinctives

1. Francis Schaeffer, *The Church Before the Watching World,* pp. 80-81.

CHAPTER 5   Contending – and the Word of God

1. Heinecken, Martin J.,*We Believe and Teach,* p. 25.
2. Terrence E. Fretheim, *Search,* Unit 9, *Deuteronomy, Joshua, Judges,* Leader's Guide Minneapolis: Augsburg Publishing House, 1984, pp. 80-81.
3. John Spong, *Rescuing the Bible from Fundamentalism,* chapter 8.
4. Ibid., p. 105.
5. Ibid., chapter 13.

6. Ibid., chapters 13 and 14.

7. Ibid., p. 25.

8. Ibid., chapter 2.

9. Jeffery L. Sheler, "Hell's sober comeback," *U.S. News & World Report,* March 25, 1993.

10. From foreword by Eugene F. Klug, in *The End of the Historical-Critical Method,* p. 9.

11. *An Inclusive Language Lectionary,* Atlanta: John Knox Press, Introduction, p. 1.

12. J.I. Packer, *Beyond the Battle for the Bible,* p.132.

13. Harold Lindsell, *The Battle for the Bible,* p. 86.

14. Ibid., p. 87.

15. Rudolf Bultmann, *Form Criticism,* chapter 2.

16. Marcus R. Braun, Lecture: "How Bible Doubting Undermines Christian Faith," delivered April 27, 1975.

17. *Lutheran Women,* February 1984, p. 29.

18. Douglas R. Groothus, *Unmasking The New Age,* p. 139.

19. Martha Sawyer Allen, "Jesus said ...or did he?" *Star Tribune,* Minneapolis, January 16, 1994.

20. Ibid.

21. Ibid.

22. Article, *St. Louis Post Dispatch,* January 8, 1994.

CHAPTER 6 Contending – Watchful for Subtle Deceptions

1. Norman L. Geisler, *In Defense of the Resurrection,* p. v.

2. Bradley P. Holt, *Thirsty For God,* p. 3.

3. Ibid., p. 67.

4. Ibid., p. 130.

5. Ibid., I , II, and back cover.

6. Ibid.

7. Ibid., p. 119.

8. Matthew Fox, *Manifesto For A Global Civilization,* p. 6.

9. Quote taken from *Under the Spell of Mother Earth* by Berit Kjos, p. 113.

10. Holt, op. cit., p.114.

11. John Cotter, *A Study in Syncretism,* p. 70.

12. Quote taken from *A Planned Deception* by Constance Cumbey, p. 105.

13. Hunt, McMahon, *The Seduction of Christianity,* p. 164.
14. Ibid., p.140.
15. Ibid.
16. Herbert W. Chilstrom, "Make Bible study a priority," *The Lutheran,* March 1994, p. 62.
17. Ibid.
18. Ibid.

CHAPTER 7   Contending — for Biblical Values

1. *The Rebirth of America,* Arthur DeMoss Foundation, 1986, p. 32.
2. *The Wall Street Journal,* February 16, 1994.
3. Enrique T. Rueda, *The Homosexual Network,* pp. 106-107.
4. *Star Tribune,* Minneapolis, April 15, 1993, p. 1.
5. Rueda, op. cit., p. 177.
6. *American Family Journal,* March 1994, p. 2.
7. House of Commons Social Services Committee, Volume 3, April 8-May13, 1987, p.147.
8. Lorraine Day, *AIDS What The Government Isn't Telling You,* p. 29.
9. Ibid., p. 8.
10. Ibid., p. 159.
11. *Florida Today,* "AIDS virus causes cancer," April 7, 1994, p. 2A.
12. Kay Miller, *Star Tribune,* Minneapolis, February 8, 1983, p. 4A.
13. *The Christian News,* April 25, 1994.
14. *The Lutheran,* October 1987, p. 29.
15. "Embracing God's World," Constituting Convention Women of the Evangelical Lutheran Church in America, June 12, 1987, distributed at Convention Workshop.
16. *Step by Step,* Week 1, p. 41.
17. *The Lutheran,* February 1994.
18. Anita Hill, *Let Justice Roll Down Like Waters,* published by ELCA, 1993.
19. *American Family Journal,* op.cit., p. 2.
20. John Leo, *US News and World Report,* March 21, 1994, p. 22.
21. *Christianity Today,* October 4, 1993.
22. Francis Schaeffer, *Whatever Happened To The Human Race,* p. 60.
23. Ibid., p. 54.

24. *U.S. News and World Report,* "Death on Trial," April 25, 1994.

25. *Family Values,* Vol. 2 - No. 2, March, April 1994.

26. *U.S. News and World Report,* op. cit.

27. Ibid.

CHAPTER 8 Contending – Against the One-World Religion

1. Peter Lalonde, *One World Under Anti-Christ,* p. 289.

2. George Cornell, "Religious Fundamentalism," *Star Tribune,* Minneapolis, April 24, 1993.

3. Joy Perry, *Wisconsin Report,* December 16, 1993.

4. Brochure, published by The Center for Spiritual Growth, Cambridge, Mn, 1994.

5. Gayda Hollnagel, *LaCross Tribune*, October 31, 1991.

6. D.L. Cuddy, "The Deceptive New Age 'Service' and 'Light'," article published 1990.

7. *Lutheran Commentator*, September/October 1993, p. 7.

8. Carl E. Braaten, "The Outrage of The Season," *Dialog,* Summer, 1990.

9. Ad for Center for Spiritual Growth, *Star Tribune,* Minneapolis, Dec. 18, 1993, p. 7 E.

10. Jeannie Williams, *USA Today,* February 23, 1993.

11. Louis M. Savory and Patricia H. Berne, *The Art of Spiritual Presence,* Ramsey, N.J.:Paulist Press, p.3.

12. Ibid., p. 163.

13. Ibid., p.170.

14. D.L. Cuddy, "The New World Order," article published 1990.

15. 1993 Parliament of World Religions Catalogue.

16. Robert Muller, *The New Genesis,* p. 64.

17. Robert Muller, *World Goodwill Newsletter,* 1994, No 1.

18. *The Lutheran,* October 1993.

19. *Christian Research Journal,* Fall 1993, p. 10.

20. *World Goodwill Newsletter,* No. 3, 1993, p. 4.

21. Ibid.

22. *CPWR Journal,* November 1993.

23. *Breakthrough News,* a publication of Global Education Associates, Winter/Spring 1994.

24. Ibid.

25. Literature furnished by Temple of Understanding.
26. Literature furnished by Thanksgiving Square Commission.
27. Muller, *The New Genesis,* p. 82.
28. *World Goodwill Newsletter,* 1993, No.3.
29. *Bimillennial Research Report,* March-April, 1992.
30. Ibid.
31. *Florida Today,* March 30, 1994, p. 3A.
32. *The Christian News,* April 4, 1994, p. 7.
33. *World,* April 9, 1994, pp. 10-13.
34. Dave Hunt, *The Berean Call,* May 1994, page 1.
35. *World,* op.cit.

CHAPTER 9 Contending – Against the One-World Government

1. D.L. Cuddy, *The New World Order, A Critique and Chronology,* p. 18.
2. From article "Beware World Government Agenda," by D.L. Cuddy, published 1994.
3. Ibid.
4. D.L. Cuddy, *An American Commentary,* p. 128.
5. D.L.Cuddy, *Now is the Dawning of the New Age New World Order,* p. 284.
6. Ibid., p. 292.
7. William F. Jasper, *Global Tyranny...Step by Step,* p. 20.
8. D. L. Cuddy, *op.cit.,* p. 296.
9. Ibid., p. 251.
10. Ibid.
11. D. L. Cuddy, article, "Beware World Government Agenda".
12. James W. Wardner, "The Planned Destruction of America," published in *News Watch Magazine,* January 1994, p. 8.
13. Ibid., p. 6.
14. Cuddy, *Now is the Dawning of the New Age New World Order,* p. 248.
15. Wardner, "The Planned Destruction of America, p. 13.
16. Ibid., p. 14.
17. Ibid.
18. Jasper, op.cit. p. 184.
19. Ibid., p. 182.
20. Ibid., p. 187.

21. Berit Kjos, Article in *The Christian World Report*, July 1993.

22. Cuddy, *op.cit.*, p. 354.

23. George W. Blount, *Peace Through World Government*, pp. 1-2.

24. Ibid., p. 88.

CHAPTER 10 Contending – Against the Feminist Onslaught

1. Expression used in the Lutheran order of Baptism.

2. Statistics taken from *Megatrends for Women*, by Aburdene and Naisbitt, p. 128.

3. Rosemary R. Reuther, *Woman Guides: Readings Toward A Feminist Theology*, Boston: Beacon Press, 1985, p. 213.

4. *Magatrends*, op.cit., p. 124.

5. Martha Sawyer Allen, "Christian feminists question meaning of atonement," *Star/Tribune*, Minneapolis, February 16, 1994.

6. Rita Nakashima Brock, tape recording of RE-Imagining Conference, Tape 2-1, Side B.

7. Martha Sawyer Allen, op.cit.

8. Ibid.

9. Elisabeth S. Florenza, *But She Said, Feminist Practices of Biblical Interpretation*, p. 23.

10. Ibid., p. 54.

11. Ibid., pp. 48-50.

12. Ibid., p. 60.

13. Ibid., pp. 28-29.

14. Ibid., p. 32.

15. Martha Sawyer Allen, Re-imagining Conference article, *Star/Tribune*, Minneapolis, November 3, 1993.

16. Ibid.

17. Ibid.

18. Steve Beard, RE-Imagining Conference Article, *American Family Journal*, February 1994.

19. Virginia Mollenkott, RE-Imagining Conference, tape recording, Tape 11-1, Side B.

20. Steve Beard, op.cit.

21. George W. Cornell, "Critics Blast Conference," *Florida Today*, January 29, 1994.

22. Lois Blinkhorn, "Today's Spiritual Women," *Milwaukee Journal*, April 11, 1993.

23. Ibid.

24. Wanda Marrs, *New Age Lies To Women,* pp. 130-131.

25. Richard N. Ostling, "When God Was a Woman," *Time*   May 6, 1991, p. 73.

CHAPTER 11 Pathways to Victory

1. Webster's New Universal Unabridged Dictionary

2. J. Oswald Sanders, *Spiritual Maturity,* Chicago: Moody Press, 1962, p. 65.

3. Francis Schaeffer, *The Great Evangelical Disaster,* p. 61.

4. *US News and World Report,* April 4, 1994, p. 50.

5. *New Testament Commentary: James, I - III John,* Grand Rapids: Baker, 1986.

6. Andrew Murray, *With Christ in the School of Prayer,* Whitaker House, 1981, p. 100.

7. Ibid., p. 115.

8. *Luther's Small Catechism,* The General Synod Edition.

BIBLIOGRAPHY

Aburdene, Patricia and Naisbitt, John *Megatrends For Women,* New York: Fawcett Columbine, 1992.

Bainton, Roland H. *Studies on the Reformation,* Boston: Beacon Press, 1966.

Blount, George W. *Peace Through World Government,* Durham, NC: Moore Publishing Co., 1974.

Bultmann, Rudolf *Jesus and the Word,* London: Charles Scribner's Sons, 1934.

Bultmann, Rudolf *Form Criticism,* New York: Harper and Brothers, originally published in 1934.

Bultmann, Rudolf *Kerygma and Myth,* New York: Harper and Brothers, 1961.

Cotter, John *A Study in Syncretism (The Background and Apparatus of the Emerging One World Church),* Flesherton, Ontario: Canadian Intelligence Publications, 1979.

Cuddy, Dennis L. *Now Is The Dawning of The New Age New World Order,* Oklahoma City: Hearthstone Publishing, 1991.

Cuddy, Dennis L. *An American Commentary,* Oklahoma City: Hearthstone Publishing, Ltd., 1993.

Cumbey, Constance E. *A Planned Deception,* East Detroit: Pointe Publishers, Inc., 1985.

Crossan, John D. *The Historical Jesus,* San Francisco: Harper, 1991.

Day, Lorraine *AIDS, What the Government Isn't Telling You,* Palm Desert, California: Rockford Press, 1991.

Du Mas, Frank M. *Gay Is Not Good,* Nashville: Thomas Nelson Publishers, 1979.

Foxe, John *Foxe's Book of English Marytrs,* Waco, Tx: Word, 1981. (Originally published in 1584.)

Florenza, Elisabeth S. *But She Said, Feminist Practices of Biblical Interpretation,* Boston: Beacon Press, 1992.

Fox, Matthew *Manifesto For A Global Civilization,* Santa Fe, New Mexico: Bear & Company, Inc., 1982.

Geisler, Norman L. *In Defense of the Resurrection,* Lynchburg, Virginia: Quest Publications, 1991.

Groothus, Douglas R. *Unmasking The New Age,* Downers Grove, Illinois: InterVarsity Press, 1986.

Heinecken, Martin J. *We Believe and Teach,* Philadelphia: Fortress Press, 1980.

Holt, Bradley P. *Thirsty For God A Brief History of Christian Spirituality,* Minneapolis: Augsburg, 1993.

Hunt, David and McMahon, T.A. *The Seduction of Christianity:* Eugene, Oregon: Harvest House, 1985.

Jasper, William F. *Global Tyranny...Step by Step,* Appleton, Wisconsin: Western Islands, 1992.

Kjos, Berit *Under the Spell of Mother Earth,* Wheaton, Illinois: Victor Books: 1992.

Koop, C. Everett, Schaeffer, Francis A. *Whatever Happened To The Human Race,* Westchester, Illinois: Crossway Books, 1983.

Lalonde, Peter *One World Under Anti-Christ,* Eugene, Oregon: Harvest House, 1991.

Latourette, Kenneth Scott *A History of Christianity,* New York: Harper & Brothers, 1953.

Lindsell, Harold *The Battle for the Bible,* Grand Rapids, Michigan: Zondervan, 1976.

Ljostveit, P. *Innermission Church History,* Hauge Lutheran Innermission Federation, 1948.

Machen, J. Gresham *The Christian Faith in the Modern World* , New York: Macmillan Company,1936.

Marrs, Wanda *New Age Lies To Women,* Austin, Texas: Living Truth Publishers, 1989.

Matrisciana, Caryl *Gods of The New Age,* Eugene, Oregon: Harvest House, 1985.

McIntire, Carl *Outside The Gate,* Collingswood, N.J.: Christian Beacon Press, 1967.

McIntire, Carl *The Death of a Church,* Collingswood, N.J.: Christian Beacon Press, 1967.

Muller, Robert *The New Genesis: Shaping a Global Spirituality,* Garden City, New York: Doubleday, Image Books ed., 1984.

Otten, Herman J. *Baal or God,* New Haven, Ms: Leader Publishing Co. 1965.

Packer, J.I. *Beyond the Battle for the Bible,* Westchester, Illinois: Cornerstone Books, 1980.

Rueda, Enrique T. *The Homosexual Network,* Old Greenwich, Connecticut: The Devin Adair Company, 1982.

Scroggs, Robin, *The New Testament and Homosexuality,* Philadelphia: Fortress Press, 1983.

Schaeffer, Edith *The Tapestry,* Waco, Tx: Word Books, 1981.

Schaeffer, Francis A. *The Church Before the Watching World,* Downers Grove, Il: InterVarsity Press, 1976.

Schaeffer, Francis A. *The Great Evangelical Disaster,* Westchester, Illinois: Crossway Books, 1984.

Sheldon, Henry C. *History of the Christian Church,* New York: Thomas Y. Crowell and Co., 1894.

Spong, John S. *Rescuing the Bible from Fundamentalism,* San Francisco: Harper San Francisco, 1992.